New Zealand
South Island

Darroch Donald

Credits

Footprint credits
Editor: Jo Williams
Production and layout: Emma Bryers
Maps: Kevin Feeney

Managing Director: Andy Riddle
Commercial Director: Patrick Dawson
Publisher: Alan Murphy
Publishing Managers: Felicity Laughton,
Jo Williams, Nicola Gibbs
Marketing and Partnerships Director:
Liz Harper
Marketing Executive: Liz Eyles
Trade Product Manager: Diane McEntee
Account Managers: Paul Bew, Tania Ross
Advertising: Renu Sibal, Elizabeth Taylor
Trade Product Co-ordinator: Kirsty Holmes

Photography credits
Front cover: Dreamstime
Back cover: Shutterstock

Printed in Great Britain by CPI Antony Rowe,
Chippenham, Wiltshire

MIX
Paper from
responsible sources
FSC
www.fsc.org   FSC® C013604

Publishing information
Footprint *Focus New Zealand South Island*
1st edition
© Footprint Handbooks Ltd
September 2012

ISBN: 978 1 908206 84 8
CIP DATA: A catalogue record for this book
is available from the British Library

® Footprint Handbooks and the Footprint
mark are a registered trademark of
Footprint Handbooks Ltd

Published by Footprint
6 Riverside Court
Lower Bristol Road
Bath BA2 3DZ, UK
T +44 (0)1225 469141
F +44 (0)1225 469461
footprinttravelguides.com

Distributed in the USA by Globe Pequot
Press, Guilford, Connecticut

The content of Footprint *Focus New Zealand
South Island* has been taken directly
from Footprint's *New Zealand* which was
researched and written by Darroch Donald.

Contents

North Cape

Waitangi
National reserve

Whangarei

Dargaville

Great Barrier Island

*Coromandel
Peninsula*

Hauraki Gulf

Auckland

Whitianga

Thames

Waikato

Tauranga

Bay of Plenty

*East
Cape*

Hamilton

Rotorua

Tasman Sea

Waitomo

Raukumara Range

Waitotapu
Thermal reserve

North Island

Gisborne

New Plymouth

Cape Egmont

Mt Egmont

Ruapehu

*Lake
Taupo*

*Hawke
Bay*

Napier

Wanganui

Ruahine Range

Palmerston North

❹ *Cape Farewell*

*Tasman
Bay*

Picton

Masterton

Tararua Range

Nelson

❸

Blenheim

□ **WELLINGTON**

Cook Strait

Cape Palliser

Mt Franklyn ▲

❷

Kaikoura

Greymouth

❶

Hokitika

Hanmer
Springs

Southern Alps

Christchurch

Mt Cook ▲

Banks Peninsula

Ashburton

Mt Aspiring ▲

Timaru

*Milford
Sound*

*Lake
Wakatipu*

Cromwell

Oamaru

Queenstown

*Lake
Te Anau*

Dunedin

Otago Peninsula

❺

Pacific Ocean

Gore

Balclutha

Invercargill

Foveaux Strait

❻

Stewart Island

N

100 km

100 miles

4 ● New Zealand South Island

The regions of Marlborough and Nelson have all the classic New Zealand ingredients – mountains, lakes, golden beaches and great tramping tracks – all warmed by the sunniest climate in the country. The inhabitants are a diverse bunch, from the farmers, fruit growers and winemakers in the valleys, to the artists and alternative lifestylers in the quiet creative havens of the Marlborough Sounds and smaller rural towns like Takaka. Despite the appealing lifestyle and obvious attractions, few foreigners have heard of this region. Most simply pass through on their way to the tourist honeypots further south, stopping only briefly in Picton, the main ferry port on the South Island.

Canterbury is the largest region in the South Island. Central Canterbury is the hub of the South Island and its capital, Christchurch, is the country's second largest city. Aesthetically and historically it is also the most Anglican as one of the first areas on the South Island settled by the British in 1850. North Canterbury is home to the thermal resort of Hanmer Springs, while beyond that is Kaikoura, famous for its whales and sea life. In South Canterbury is MacKenzie Country, with the region's most stunning and diverse scenery, culminating in Pukaki Lake and New Zealand's highest peak, Mount Cook (3754 m). West of Christchurch, beyond the curtain of mountains, is the 'wild' West Coast, with breathtaking scenery.

Otago is both diverse and stunning with mountain ranges in the west, barren and expansive landscapes in Central Otago and green rolling hills and beaches of the Otago Peninsula. Dunedin, the capital, retains much of its Scottish heritage and a grandeur borne of the gold booms of the 19th century. With the Otago Peninsula on its doorstep and the diverse and rare wildlife that thrives there, it is also known as the wildlife capital of the country. Queenstown, with over 150 activities on offer, is seen as the adventure capital of the world. Otago's neighbour, Southland, has the most spectacular yet inaccessible landscapes in the country. Half the coast is mountainous, remote and inhospitable. The other half is home to Southland's largest town, Invercargill, and the beautiful Catlin Coast.

Planning your trip

Getting to New Zealand

Being an island nation and 'last stop from anywhere', the majority of international visitors arrive by air and in to Auckland New Zealand's largest city and airport. Over recent years cruise ship visits have increased, but passengers are tied to a limited onshore itinerary.

Air

From Europe The main route is usually via Heathrow or Frankfurt, either west with a stopover in the USA (Los Angeles), or east with stopovers in Southeast Asia or the Middle East. The Australasian airline market is currently very volatile and prices vary. The cheapest return flights, off-season (May-August), will be around £800 (€931), rising to at least £1100 (€1281) around Christmas. Mainstream carriers include **Air New Zealand** ① *airnewzealand.com*, and **Qantas** ① *qantas.com* (west via the USA); and **Singapore Airlines** ① *singapore air.com*; **Thai Air** ① *thaiair.com*; **Air Malaysia** ① *malaysiaairlines. com*, and **Emirates** ① *emirates.com* (all east via Asia, or the Middle East). As usual the best bargains are to be found online.

From the Americas Competition is fierce with several operators including **Air New Zealand** ① *airnewzealand.com*; **Qantas** ① *qantas.com*; **Air Canada** ① *aircanada.com* and **Lufthansa** ① *lufthansa.com*, all offering flights from Los Angeles (LAX) or San Francisco (SFO) to Auckland. One of the cheapest is the new Richard Branson venture **VAustralia** ① *vaustralia.com.au*, that offers good deals via Sydney. **Air Canada** ① *aircanada.com*, and **United** ① *united.com*, connecting with Alliance partners at LAX fly from Vancouver, Toronto and Montreal. Prices range from CAN$1650-2700. There are also direct flights from Buenos Aires to Auckland with **Aerolíneas Argentinas**, aerolineas.com.ar, flying out of New York and Miami.

The cost of a standard return in the low season (May-August) from LAX starts from around US$1050, from New York from US$1500 and Chicago from US$1450. In the high season add about US$300 to the standard fare.

The flight time between LAX and Auckland is around 12½ hours.

From Australia As you might expect there is a huge choice and much competition with trans-Tasman flights, in fact it is corporate warfare. Traditionally most flights used to go from Cairns, Brisbane, Sydney and Melbourne to Auckland but now many of the cheaper flights can actually be secured to Wellington, Christchurch, Dunedin and Queenstown.

Flights and especially ski package deals to Queenstown can also be cheaper and have been heavily promoted in recent years, but conditions usually apply, giving you limited flexibility. At any given time there are usually special deals on offer from the major players like **Qantas** ① *qantas.com.au*; Qantas subsidiary **JetStar** ① *jetstar.com.au*; **Air New Zealand** ① *airnewzealand.com.au*, and **Pacific Blue** ① *pacificblue.com.au*, so again shop around and online. Prices range from AUS$270-750 return. The flight time between Sydney and Auckland is three hours, Melbourne three hours 45 minutes.

Don't miss...

Airport information The two principal international airports in New Zealand are **Auckland** ① *T0800 247767, auckland-airport.co.nz*, in the North Island and **Christchurch** ① *T64 3353 7774, christchurch-airport.co.nz*, in the South. Auckland is by far the most utilized and better served of the two with direct flights worldwide, while Christchurch deals mainly with connecting flights via or to Australia. Additionally, Wellington, Dunedin and Queenstown also serve the East Coast of Australia.

Auckland airport is 21 km south of the city centre. **Shuttle bus** ① *airbus.co.nz*, or taxis are the main transport services to the city and they depart regularly from outside the terminal building. The airbus will cost about $15 one-way $22 return, a taxi around $60. There is no rail link.

Transport in New Zealand

Public transport in all its forms (except rail) is generally both good and efficient. All the main cities and provincial towns can be reached easily by air or by road. Although standard fares can be expensive there are a vast number of discount passes and special seasonal deals available, aimed particularly at the young independent traveller. Although it is entirely possible to negotiate the country by public transport, for sheer convenience you are advised to get your own set of wheels. Fuel prices compare favourably to most of Europe ($2.20 for unleaded, $1.50 for diesel).

Air
Domestic air travel If you do not have your own hired or private vehicle then at least a few domestic flights are worth considering, especially between the islands. Currently **Air New Zealand** ① *T0800-737000, airnewzealand.co.nz*; Qantas subsidiary **Jetstar** ① *T0800-800995, jetstar.com*; and **Pacific Blue** ① *T0800-670000, pacificblue.co.nz*, are the principal air carriers providing services between Auckland, Christchurch and Wellington and most regional centres. A one-way ticket from Auckland to Christchurch can be bought online for as little as $50.

Road
Bus National bus travel in New Zealand is well organized and the networks and daily schedules are good. Numerous shuttle companies service the South Island and there are also many local operators and independent companies that provide shuttles to accommodation establishments, attractions and activities. These are listed in the Transport sections of the main travelling text.

The main bus company is **Intercity** ① *intercitycoach.co.nz*. For information and reservations call Christchurch T03-365 1113. Also popular are **Nakedbus.com**, which uses the same model of low overheads and internet-only booking service that the cheap airlines do. It has managed to undercut long-established companies.

All the major companies offer age, student and backpacker concessions as well as a wide variety of flexible national or regional travel passes with some in combination with the interisland ferry and rail.

Car Other than a campervan this is by far the best way to see New Zealand. Most major international hire companies and many national companies are in evidence. You may also consider buying a vehicle for the trip and selling it again afterwards but research prices thoroughly and get the vehicle independently checked by the AA (aa.co.nz). There are specialist markets in both Auckland and Christchurch (backpackerscarmarket.co.nz).

A hire vehicle will give you the flexibility and freedom needed to reach the more remote and beautiful places. Outside the cities traffic congestion and parking is rarely a problem. In New Zealand you drive on the left (though most Aucklanders drive where they like). Make sure you familiarize yourself with the rules before setting out (NZ Road Code booklets are available from AA offices). The speed limit on the open road is 100 kph and in built-up areas it is 50 kph. Police patrol cars and speed cameras are omnipresent so if you speed you will almost certainly be caught. A valid driving license from your own country or an international license is required and certainly must be produced if you rent a vehicle. Parking in the cities can be very expensive. Do not risk parking in restricted areas or exceeding your time allotment on meters. Finally, never leave or hide valuables in your car and lock it at all times.

If you are travelling in a bought second-hand vehicle you are advised to join **The New Zealand Automobile Association (AA)** ① *T09-966 8800, T0800-500555, aa.co. nz; breakdowns, T0800-500222*. It also provides a great range of maps and travelling information as well as the usual member benefits. The annual membership fee of around $80 will provide basic breakdown assistance.

Good private deals can be secured with second-hand vehicles through trademe.co.nz but always get a car checked mechanically by an independent entity and do a police check for previous fines, etc (aa.co.nz).

Motor homes New Zealand is well geared up for campervan hire and travel and there's an accompanying glut of reputable international companies. Being a fairly compact country it is certainly a viable way to explore with complete independence. Although hire costs may seem excessive, once you subtract the inevitable costs of accommodation, provided you are not alone and can share those costs, it can work out cheaper in the long run. You will find that motor camps are available even in the more remote places and a powered site will cost $20-30 per night for two people. Note that lay-by parking is illegal and best avoided. Again, like car rental rates, campervan rates vary and are seasonal. Costs are rated on a sliding scale according to model, season and length of hire. The average daily charge for a basic two-berth/six-berth for hire over 28 days, including insurance is $195/295 in the high season and $75/120 in the low season. The average campervan works out at about 14-16 litres per 100 km in petrol costs. Diesel is cheaper than petrol but at present more harmful to the environment.

The most popular rental firms are **Jucy** ① *T0800-399736, T09-374 4360, jucy.co.nz*; **Maui/Britz** ① *T0800-651080, T00-800-20080801, maui.co.nz, britz.co.nz*; **Kea Campers** ① *T0800-*

520052, T09-4417833, keacampers.com, and for more unconventional vehicles, **Spaceships** ① *T0800-SPACE SHIPS, T09-5262130, spaceships.tv*, which offers Toyota People Movers or campervan hybrids complete with DVD and double bed.

Ferry

Other than a few small harbour-crossing vehicle ferries and the short trip to Stewart Island from Bluff in Southland, the main focus of ferry travel is of course the inter-island services across Cook Strait. The two ports are Wellington at the southern tip of the North Island and Picton in the beautiful Marlborough Sounds on the South Island.

There are two services: the **Interislander** ① *T0800-802802, T04-4983302, interislander. co.nz*, and the smaller of the two companies **Bluebridge** ① *T0800-844844, T04-4716188, bluebridgeco.nz*.

A standard vehicle with two passengers will cost about $265 one-way, a motor home with two passengers $365 and two passengers no vehicle $53 per person.

Train

For years the rail network in New Zealand has struggled to maintain anything other than a core network between its main population centres. However, that said, the trains in themselves are pretty comfortable, the service is good and the stunning scenery will soon take your mind off things. Within the South Island, the daily services between Picton and Christchurch (the TranzCoastal and Christchurch to Greymouth (the TranzAlpine) are both world-class journeys. For detail contact **TranzScenic** ① *T0800-872467, T04-4950775, tranzscenic.co.nz*.

Also, designed specifically as a tourist attraction, the **Taieri Gorge Railway** ① *T03-477 4449, taieri.co.nz*, runs from Dunedin to Middlemarch and back, with shuttle connections to Queenstown.

All fares are of a single class, but prices range greatly from 'standard' to 'super saver' so check carefully what you are entitled to and what deals you can secure.

Where to stay in New Zealand

New Zealand offers the full range of tourist accommodation from exclusive luxury lodges to basic campsites. Indeed, such is the sheer variety that the only limitation beyond the budget is your own imagination.

Given the compact nature of the country, its modern infrastructure and in no small part its awesome natural aesthetics, many choose the independent option and hire a motor home or a campervan, or if on a limited budget purchase a vehicle temporarily for the trip. Then, by staying predominantly at motor parks, flexibility and freedom can be maximised. This is by far the best and most popular option in New Zealand and the kiwi tourism industry is well geared up for it.

But whatever accommodation you choose you will find a huge range on offer with the local and regional visitor information centres (i-SITES) or internet being the best places to both source and to book. There are also many books available including the AA accommodation guides (aaguides.co.nz) as well as numerous motor parks, motels, campsites and backpacker guides.

In the high season (November to March) and particularly around Christmas and the first two weeks in January you are advised to book all types of accommodation at least three days in advance.

Price codes

Where to stay

$$$$	more than $200 per night		$$$	$100-200
$$	$50-100		$	under $50

Price is for a double room in high season.

Restaurants

$$$	more than $30	$$	$20-30	$	under $20

Price is per person for a 2-course meal with a drink, including service and cover charge.

Hotels

Hotels in New Zealand can generally be listed under one of four categories: large luxury hotels; chain hotels; boutique hotels; and budget hotels.

There are plenty of luxurious (four- to five-star) hotels in the major cities and prices range from $250-1000 per night. As you would expect, all rooms are equipped with the latest technology. They also have restaurants and leisure facilities including swimming pools, spa pools and gyms.

Standard chain hotels are commonplace, vary in both age and quality and include names such as Quality Hotels, Novotel and Copthorne. Found in all major cities and the larger provincial towns, their standard prices range from $130-300 but they have regular weekend or off-season deals. Most have restaurants, pools and a gym.

Boutique hotels vary in size and price but tend to be modern and of a luxurious standard. The smaller, more intimate boutique hotels are overtaking the major chains in popularity. On average double rooms here can cost anything from $175-400.

Given the flourishing backpacker industry in New Zealand, budget hotels struggle to exist and most often you will find the generic title equates to exactly that.

Lodges and B&Bs

There are a growing number of luxury lodges throughout the country and most sell themselves on their location as much as their architecture, sumptuous rooms, facilities and cuisine. Prices tend to be high, ranging from $200 to a mind-bending $2600 per night (which equates to almost eight months in a well-equipped motor park). B&Bs are not as common in New Zealand as they are in Europe, but can still be found in most places. They vary greatly in style, size and quality and can be anything from a basic double room with shared bathroom and a couple of boiled eggs for breakfast to a luxurious ensuite or self-contained unit with the full cooked breakfast. Again prices vary, with the standard cost being as little as $75-100. Many lodges and B&Bs also offer evening meals. Again, the visitor information centres (i-SITES) are the best place to both source and book.

Home and farmstays

Generally speaking if an establishment advertises itself as a homestay it will deliberately lack the privacy of the standard B&B and you are encouraged to mix with your hosts. The idea is that you get an insight into Kiwi life, but it may or may not be for you depending on your preferences and personality.

Farmstays of course give you the added agricultural and rural edge, and are generally recommended. Accommodation can take many forms from being in-house with your

Qualmark...

The Qualmark star grading system, which is the official tourist operator star grading system in New Zealand, can help you choose the type of accommodation you are looking for, in the style that suits you. It ranges from 1 star (Acceptable), through 5 stars (Exceptional), with an additional category 'Exclusive' (Outstanding). Look out for the black and yellow signs with silver fern logo.

hosts or fully self-contained, and breakfasts and evening meals are often optional. You may find yourself helping to round up sheep or milking a cow and if you have kids (farmstays usually welcome them) they will be wonderfully occupied for hours.

Both homestays and farmstays tend to charge the same, or slightly lower, rates as B&Bs. **New Zealand Farm Holidays** ① *T09-412 9649, nzfarmholidays.co.nz*, based near Auckland, produces a helpful free catalogue listing about 300 establishments.

Motels

Motels are still the preferred option of the average Kiwi holidaymaker and business traveller. They are everywhere and reproducing furtively. They vary greatly, from the awful, stained 1950s love shacks to the new and luxurious condos with bubbly spa pool. There is usually a range of rooms available and almost all have at least a shower, kitchen facilities and a TV – though whether it actually works and has Sky TV (or doubles as a plant pot) depends on the price. Most are clean, comfortable and well appointed, while in others you may find yourself trying to sleep next to the main road. Prices vary from studio units at about $75-85, one-bedroom units from $85-120 and suites accommodating families and groups for an additional charge for each adult. Many of the bigger and better establishments have a restaurant and a swimming pool. Many also make the most of the country's thermal features and have spas, sometimes even in your room.

Hostels

New Zealand is well served with hostels and budget accommodation establishments. Naturally, they vary greatly in age, design, location and quality. Some enjoy a busy atmosphere in the centre of town while others provide a quiet haven in the country. They also have a range of types of bedrooms on offer, with many having separate double and single rooms as well as the traditional dormitory. Dorms are usually single sex but sometimes optionally mixed. Camping facilities within the grounds are also common. Generally, hostels are good places to meet other travellers, managers are usually very knowledgeable and helpful; pick-ups are often free. Bikes, kayaks or other activity gear can often be hired at low cost or are free to use. Wherever you stay you will have access to equipped kitchens, a laundry, games or TV room, plenty of local information and, of course, phones and the internet. Prices vary little for a dorm bed, from $20 depending on season. Single rooms and doubles tend to be around $55, or about $30 per adult. In the high season and especially over Christmas through to March you are advised to pre-book everywhere at least three days in advance.

There are several major backpacking membership organizations in New Zealand that provide hostel listings and discounts.

Budget Backpacker Hostels Ltd (BBH) ① *T03-379 3014, bbh.co.nz*, has around 350 member establishments that must meet certain minimum quality criteria. These are listed in its Blue Book (free from i-SITES) along with handy descriptions, contact details and location maps of each hostel.

The **YHA (Youth Hostel Association NZ)** ① *T0800-278299/T03-379 9970, yha.co.nz*, is part of a worldwide organization and they have about 70 establishments throughout New Zealand; the vast majority are associates as opposed to YHA owned and operated. Being part of a large organization, most are on a par if not better than the independent backpacker hostels. They all offer very much the same in standard of accommodation and facilities. They are also to be congratulated on their intensive eco-friendly policies with recycling not only provided in most hostels, but actively and enthusiastically embraced.

YHAs are only open to members but you can join in your home country (if YHA exists) or in New Zealand for an annual fee of $40 ($30 for renewals). Non-members can also stay at hostels for an additional charge of $3 per night. YHA membership cards can also entitle you to a number of discounts, including up to 30% off air and bus travel. Pick up the YHA Accommodation and Hostel Guide at any major i-SITE visitor centre.

Motor parks camps and cabins

New Zealand's fairly compact size and quality road network lends itself to road touring and it is very well served with quality motor parks and campsites. In fact, it is hailed as one of the best in the world. Motor parks can be found almost everywhere and not necessarily just in towns. The quality and age does of course vary. Some are modern and well equipped while others are basic. Almost all motor parks have laundry facilities and a few will charge a small fee ($0.20-1) for hot showers. Prices are generally very reasonable and range from $10-15 per person (child half price) for non-powered sites. Powered sites are often the same price or a few dollars more.

Most motor parks have a range of cabins from dog kennels to well-appointed alpine-type huts. They vary in price starting with a standard cabin with little more than a bed and electric socket for a mere $35 to a cabin with better facilities for up to $60 per night (for two) with an additional charge of $12-15 per person after that.

The **Top Ten** chain of motor parks, which has almost 50 nationwide, though up to $3 more expensive per night, is generally highly recommended (top10.co.nz).

Wild camping

'Where can I camp?' 'Assume nothing – always ask a local' is the catch-cry of the authorities and rightly so – wild camping with no respect for property and environment is not tolerated. The best advice is to stick to designated sites and to source them ask at the local visitor information centre (i-SITE), or regional Department of Conservation (DoC) office (doc.govt.nz). The website camping.org.nz is also useful.

The DoC has more than 100 basic campsites all over the country with many being in prime locations. They tend to provide clean running water, toilet facilities and BBQ areas, but rarely allow open fires. The national parks in particular are all excellently facilitated with comfortable well-equipped huts. There is usually a nightly fee of $2-10. Fees for huts are anything from $5-40 per night depending on category and location. If you plan to use DoC campsites and huts you are advised to research their locations, fee structures, rules and regulations and book well in advance.

Food and drink in New Zealand

Budget permitting, you are in for a treat. The quality of food in New Zealand is superb. Although there are many types of traditional cuisine and restaurants in evidence, the principal style is Pacific Rim. It dips into the culinary heritage of many of the cultures of the Oceania region as well as further afield like Europe. For dishes that have a distinctly Kiwi edge look out for the lamb (arguably the best in the world), pork, venison and freshwater fish like salmon or trout – though note you cannot buy trout commercially.

As you might expect there is also a heavy emphasis on seafood. The choice is vast with many warm-water fish like snapper of particular note. Other seafood delights include crayfish (the South Pacific equivalent to the lobster), oysters, paua (abalone), scallops and the famous green-lipped mussels. There are also some treats in store from below the ground. The kumara (sweet potato) will shed a whole new light on the humble spud, while many of the international vegetables like asparagus and broccoli come cheap (especially while in season) and are always fresh. From the tree the fruit of choice is of course the succulent kiwi fruit, which although not exclusively grown in New Zealand is deservedly celebrated. A traditional dessert in New Zealand is the pavlova; a sort of mountainous cake made of meringue and whipped cream. For a real traditional treat try a Maori *hangi* or feast. Prepared properly and without ketchup you will be amazed at just how good and different fish, meat and vegetables can taste when cooked underground.

Eating out

There are eateries to suit every taste and budget from the ubiquitous fast-food joints to world-class seafood restaurants. Auckland and Wellington (the latter has more cafés and restaurants per capita than New York) are particularly rich in choice with a vast selection of cafés, café-bars, brasseries and specialist international restaurants giving added puff to the celebrated Pacific Rim.

Eating out in New Zealand is generally good value, especially given the usually favourable foreign exchange rates. The vast majority of eateries fall into the 'mid-range' bracket ($18-25 for a main). Most cafés open for breakfast between 0700 and 0900 and stay open until at least 1700, and often until late into the evening or the early hours. This usually applies seven days a week with special Sunday brunch hours provided. Most mid-range restaurants open their doors daily for lunch (often 1100-1400) and dinner (from 1800). The more exclusive establishments usually open for dinner from about 1800, with some (especially in winter) only opening some weekday evenings and at weekend

Vegetarians are generally well catered for in the main centres and provincial towns.

Self-catering

If you intend to do your own cooking, supermarkets offer a wide choice of fare and are often open until around 2200. The main chains include Big Fresh, Woolworths and New World, with Pac-n-Save and Countdown being marginally cheaper. For fresh fruit and vegetables, stick to the numerous roadside or wholesale fruit markets where the difference in price and quality can be astonishing. If touring via motor parks always check to see if they have camp kitchen facilities as standards vary.

Drinks

Other than 'L&P' (a fairly unremarkable soft drink hailing from Paeroa in the Waikato, North Island) New Zealand lacks a national drink. If there is one, it is the highly sub-standard and over-rated beer called Lion Red or branded bottled beers like 'Steinlager'. Rest assured, however, that all the main internationally well-known bottled beers are available, as are some good foreign tap ales like Guinness.

Beer and lager is usually sold by the 'handle', the 'glass' (pint) or the 'jug' (up to three pints). Half-pints come in a 12-fl oz (350 ml) glass. Rarely is a pint a proper imperial pint, it's usually just under. Drinks generally cost $7-8 for a pint, about $5-6 for a jug of cheaper domestic beers and up to $8 for a double shot of spirit. Alcohol is much cheaper in rural pubs and RSAs (Retired Servicemen's Associations), where you can usually get yourself signed in. The minimum drinking age has just been reduced from 21 to 18. Liquor shops (off licenses) are everywhere and alcohol can generally (in most places) be bought seven days a week. There is also a thriving coffee culture almost everywhere in the main towns and cities, so you will not go without your daily caffeine fix.

New Zealand's diversity of climates and soil types has borne an equally rich array of wines and after over a century of development the country now boasts many internationally recognized labels. Hawke's Bay and Nelson/Marlborough areas are the principal wine-producing regions. New Zealand Sauvignon Blanc is rated throughout the world as one of the best, but there is growing recognition for its Chardonnay, Pinot Noir, Cabernet Sauvignon and Merlot. The choice is vast and whether a connoisseur or a novice you are advised to experiment. If you can, visit one of the many vineyards that offer tastings and cellar sales. For more information about New Zealand wines refer to nzwine. com or winesnewzealand.co.nz.

Entertainment in New Zealand

Despite the diminishing and undeserved reputation as a cultural backwater, New Zealand's entertainment scene is fresh and exciting. The major centres all boast numerous contemporary and historical venues that vie for a host of first-class domestic and international concerts and shows. Theatre, orchestral concerts, ballet, dance, comedy, rock and jazz are all well represented and annual or biennial festivals often attract well-known international acts. On a smaller scale you will find a vibrant nightlife in New Zealand cities and major provincial towns. Although not necessarily world class, the nightclubs, cabarets, pubs and local rock concerts will certainly have you shaking your pants. There's even Country and Western and line dancing. New Zealand also boasts two large, modern, 24-hour casinos in Christchurch. Ticketek are the national administrators for information and ticketing and a full listing of shows and events can be sourced from their website, ticketek.co.nz or nzlive.com. The local press and national newspapers also have comprehensive entertainment events listings particularly at weekends (nzherald.co.nz).

Pubs and bars

The pub scene has come on in leaps and bounds over the last decade with new establishments opening up almost everywhere and shaking off the basic tavern and hotel image. Before the 1990s the vast majority of pubs in New Zealand were the archetypal male bastions and the type of establishments where ashtrays were built into the tables, pictures of the local hairy rugby team adorned the walls and the average Saturday night consisted of a good argument about sport, a band playing Deep Purple's Smoke on the Water, followed by a fight, copious wall-to-wall vomiting and a failed attempt to get home. Of course such places still exist in some rural outposts, but generally speaking, pubs and bars are now a much more refined and classy affair, yet still retain that congenial and laid-back traditional pub atmosphere. New Zealand has also caught on to the pseudo Irish pub fad and although some are gimmicky, others are very good, offering fine surroundings and beer to match. Many drinking establishments are also now attached to restaurants and cafés with outdoor seating. In December 2004 it became illegal to smoke in all pubs, restaurants and cafés in New Zealand, though many still provide segregated (legal) areas outside. Pubs and bars are generally open from 1100-2230 with many having an extended license to 2400 and sometimes even 0300 at weekends.

Clubs

The cities and major towns all have their fair share of nightclubs that consistently pump up the volume to whatever is the latest international vibe. Some, particularly in Auckland, often attract touring international DJs.

The central business district obviously contains the most venues and a good idea for sourcing the best is to ask the staff at the largest backpacker establishments, or the barmen and women of the classiest bars. There is often a cover charge and dress is smart casual.

Gay and lesbian

Like their trans-Tasman counterparts, New Zealand cities have a welcome and thriving gay scene and the nightclubs and bars.

There are a number of specialist publications and independent groups to source the latest news, events and information, including gaypages.co.nz, pinkpagesnet.com/newzealand, gaynewzealand.com and gaytravelnet.com/nz.

Publications to look out for in the main centres include the long-established **Gay Express** (gayexpress.co.nz).

Music concerts and festivals

Many international rock stars now include at least one gig in Auckland in their itinerary, often as an adjunct to Australian gigs and they are easily accommodated in the outdoor sports stadiums or purpose-built facilities. The country also has its fair share of city- and region-based music festivals.

Festivals in New Zealand

A huge range of events and festivals are held throughout the year. i-SITES have listings of events and the NZTB website, purenz.com, or nzlive.com, have detailed nationwide events listings.

Jan

World Buskers Festival (Christchurch) worldbuskersfestival.com. Circus, street and comedic talent from around the world.

Feb

Wine Marlborough Festival wine-marlborough-festival.co.nz. Annual 3-day celebration of wine, food and fashion in New Zealand best-known wine region. **The Speight's Coast to Coast** coasttocoast.

co.nz. A grueling multi-sport event with around 800 hardy souls traversing 243 km of the South Island's rugged terrain from Hokitika on the Tasman to Christchurch on the Pacific, with a combination of running, kayaking and cycling.

Mar

Wildfoods Festival (Hokitika) wildfoods. co.nz. Attracting around 13,000 people annually, this is an extravaganza of gourmet bush tucker based on natural (or unusual) food resources from the land and sea. How about a little wasp larvae ice cream, or some vegan gonads perhaps? There's also a lot of beer on offer to wash it all down.

May
New Zealand International Comedy Festival comedyfestival.co.nz. Held simultaneously over 3 weeks in Auckland and Wellington and featuring well-known and emerging domestic and international talent.

Jun
New Zealand Gold Guitar Awards (Gore) goldguitars.co.nz. After 36 years this has become a small, yet internationally recognized, festival and competition attracting over 700 competitors.

Jul
Carrot Carnival (Ohakune) ohakune.info. And why not!

Queenstown Winter Festival
winterfestival.co.nz. Dubbed New Zealand's biggest winter party, this is a 10-day celebration of the famous activity capital's culture and community, with street parties, fireworks, music and of course plenty of on-the-piste mountain mayhem.

Aug
Christchurch Arts Festival artsfestival. co.nz. The South Islands largest, with 18 days of arts, culture and entertainment across the city. It is biennial staged rather unusually in winter and in 'odd' years.

Nov
Oamaru Victorian Heritage Celebrations Held annually in and around the elegant historical precinct of Oamaru in coastal Otago, this is a weekend event of theatre and costume, with many appropriate (and authentic) historical props, from penny-farthings to steaming traction engines.

Essentials A-Z

Children

Families and travellers with children will generally find New Zealand very child friendly and replete with all the usual concessions for travel and activities. With so many outdoor activities safety is a natural concern, but this is nothing common sense can't take care of.

There are a few hotels that will not accept children especially some of the higher end boutique B&Bs or lodges. Check in advance.

A good resource is **Kids Friendly New Zealand**, kidsfriendlynz.com. Also, in Queenstown and Wanaka look out for the independent magazine **Kidz Go**, kidz go.co. nz, available from the i-SITE visitor centres.

Customs and immigration

All visitors must have a passport valid for 3 months beyond the date you intend to leave the country. Australian citizens or holders of an Australian returning resident visa can stay in New Zealand indefinitely. UK citizens do not need a visa and are automatically issued with a 6-month visitor permit upon arrival. US, Canadian and other countries with a 'visa waiver' agreement with NZ also do not need a visa for stays of up to 3 months. Other visitors making an application for a visitor permit require: (a) a passport that is valid for at least 3 months after your departure from New Zealand; (b) an onward or return ticket to a country you have permission to enter; (c) sufficient money to support yourself during your stay (approximately NZ$1000 per month).

New Zealand Immigration Service (NZIS) T09-914 4100, T0508-558855, immigration.govt.nz.

Disabled travellers

Most public facilities are well geared up for wheelchairs, however older accommodation establishments and some public transport systems (especially rural buses) are not so well organized. It is a requirement by law to have disabled facilities in new buildings. Most airlines (both international and domestic) are generally well equipped. Disabled travellers usually receive discounts on travel fares and some admission charges. Parking concessions are also available for the disabled and temporary cards can be issued on production of a mobility card or medical certificate.

For more information within New Zealand contact: **New Zealand Disability Resource Centre**, 14 Erson Av, PO Box 24-042 Royal Oak, Auckland, T09-625 8069, disabilityresource.org.nz.

Accessible Kiwi Tours Ltd, T07-362 7622, toursnz.com, is a specialist tour company acting specifically for the disabled, based in Rotorua in the Bay of Plenty.

Emergency

Compared to some countries the average Kiwi 'bobby' is amicable, personable and there to help, not intimidate. For police, fire or ambulance: T111. Make sure you obtain police/medical reports required for insurance claims.

Health

No vaccinations are required to enter the country but you are advised to make sure your tetanus booster is up to date.

The standards of public and private medical care are generally high, but it is important to note that these services are not free. Health insurance is recommended. A standard trip to the doctor will cost around $60 with prescription charges on top of that. Dentists and hospital services are expensive. New Zealand's Accident Compensation Commission (acc.co.nz) provides limited treatment coverage for visitors but it is no substitute for travel/health insurance.

Other than the occasional crazed driver or banking CEO, there are few dangerous creatures in New Zealand with no snakes, crocodiles and so on. Although not poisonous, the dreaded sandfly is common particularly in the wetter and coastal areas of the South Island. These black, pinhead sized 'flying fangs' can annoy you beyond belief. There are numerous environmentally friendly repellents available at pharmacies.

Giardia is a water-borne bacterial parasite on the increase in New Zealand, which, if allowed to enter your system, will cause wall-to-wall vomiting, diarrhoea and rapid weight loss. Don't drink water from lakes, ponds or rivers without boiling it first.

The sun is dangerous and you should take extra care. Ozone depletion is heavy in the more southern latitudes and the incidence of melanomas and skin cancer is above average. Burn times, especially in summer, are greatly reduced so get yourself a silly hat and wear lots of sun block.

New Zealand's weather, especially at higher elevations, is changeable and can be deadly.If you are tramping, or going 'bush' make sure you are properly clothed, take maps, a first-aid kit and a compass. Above all inform somebody of your intentions.

Internet

New Zealand had one of the highest per capita internet access rates in the developed world. Internet cafés and terminals are everywhere and if you are amongst the many who start losing it if you do not get your daily email fix you should be fine. As well as internet cafés, libraries and i-SITES are a good bet, they charge standard rates of $8-$12 per hr. Due to growing competition, rates are getting cheaper, sometimes as little as $3 per hr, but shop around. The website internet-cafe-guide. com is useful for sourcing outlets.

Money

For up-to-date exchange rates, see xe.com.

The New Zealand currency is the dollar ($), divided into 100 cents (c). Coins come in denominations of 5c, 10c, 20c, 50c, $1 and $2. Notes come in $5, $10, $20, $50 and $100 denominations.

The safest way to carry money is in Traveller's Cheques (TCs). These are available for a small commission from all major banks. American Express (Amex), Visa and Thomas Cook cheques are widely accepted. Most banks do not charge for changing TCs and usually offer the best exchange rates. Keep a record of your cheque numbers and keep the cheques you have cashed separate from the cheques themselves, so that you can get a full refund of all uncashed cheques. It is best to bring NZ$ cheques to avoid extra exchange costs.

All the major credit cards are widely accepted.Most hotels, shops and petrol stations use EFTPOS (Electronic Funds Transfer at Point of Sale), meaning you don't have to carry lots of cash. It is best suited to those who have a bank account in New Zealand, but credit cards can be used with the relevant pin number. If you intend to stay in New Zealand for a while you may be able to open an account with a major bank and secure an EFTPOS/ATM card and PIN. ATMs are readily available in almost all towns and though they accept non-host bankcards, it's best to stick to your own bank's ATMs so you do not incur hidden fees. Credit cards can of course be used and some banks are linked to foreign savings accounts and cards by such networks as Cirrus and Plus.

Almost all towns and villages have at least one of the major bank branches. The main banks are the Bank of New Zealand (BNZ), the National Bank of New Zealand, the ASB Bank, Post Bank and Countrywide Bank with other trans-Tasman banks, like Westpac Trust and ANZ also in evidence. Bank opening hours are Mon-Fri 0900-1630 with some city branches opening on Sat until

1230. If you need money quickly or in an emergency the best way is to have it wired to you via any major bank with **Western Union** (NZ) T1800- 3256000, westernunion. com; or via **Thomas Cook** and **Moneygram** (NZ) T0800-872893, thomascook.com.

Cost of travelling

For a couple travelling in a campervan, self-catering and eating out occasionally and with an organized mid-range $ activity every 3rd day you will need a minimum of NZ$300 a day. Petrol is not too expensive at around NZ$1.60 per litre (NZ$6 per gallon). It is possible to survive on NZ$80 per person at motor parks with your own jalopy. But that is with no eating out, or activity costs.

Opening hours

Opening times are similar to Europe and the US. In the high season (Nov-Mar) shops generally remain open 7 days a week (0900-1700 or 1730; tourist-oriented outlets often remain open in the evening), banks and post offices open at least Mon-Fri, and 24-hr food stores are common in the main centres.

Post

Post offices (most often called Post Shops) are generally open Mon-Fri 0900-1700, Sat 0900-1230. Within New Zealand standard (local) post costs 50c for medium letters and postcards (2-3 days); $1 for airmail (fast post) to domestic centres (1-2 days); $1.80 for airmail letters to Australia and $1.80 for postcards worldwide and $2.30 for standard overseas airmail letters to Europe, North America, East Asia, Australia and South Pacific. Domestic mail takes 1-2 days, perhaps longer in rural areas. When sending any cards or letters overseas be sure to use the free blue 'Air Economy' stickers. Books of stamps are readily available as are pre-paid envelopes and a range of purpose-built cardboard boxes. Average international

delivery times vary depending on the day of the week posted, but a standard letter to the UK can take as few as 4 days (scheduled 6-12 days). North America is scheduled 4-12 days and Australia and the South Pacific 3-8 days. Post Restante services are available in most of the main centres. For details see nzpost.co.nz.

Smoking

It is illegal to smoke in bars, restaurants and the work place, except in the outdoor segregated sections, if provided. Smoking is not allowed on any public transport.

Telephone

The international code for New Zealand is 64. Within New Zealand there are 5 area codes: Auckland and Northland 09; Bay of Plenty, Coromandel, Taupo, Ruapehu and Waikato 07; Eastland, Hawkes Bay, Wanganui and Taranaki 06; Wellington 04; South Island 03. All telephone numbers in this book include the area code.

Telecom payphones are found throughout the country and are colour coded. Although there are both coin (blue) and credit card (yellow) booths available, the vast majority are phone-card only so you are advised to stock up. Cards come in $5, $10, $20 and $50 and are available from many retail outlets, visitor information offices and hostels. Unless you want to see just how fast digital numbers can disappear on screen, do not use these Telecom cards for anything other than domestic calls within New Zealand.

There are a wealth of cheap international calling cards and call centres available. One of the best is **E Phone** eph.co.nz, a calling card that accesses the net through an 0800 number. The cards vary in price from $10-$50 and can be bought from many retail outlets (look for the flag signs outside the shops). They can be used from any landline telephone. Voice instructions will tell you what to do and how much credit you have available before each call.

Local non-business calls are free from standard telephones in New Zealand, so it is not too offensive to ask to use a host's or friend's domestic (non-business) telephone. 0800 or occasionally 0508 precede toll-free calls. Try to avoid 0900 numbers as they are usually very expensive. The 2 major mobile service providers are **Telecom**, telecom.co.nz and **Vodafone**, vodafone.co.nz. Reciprocal arrangements are in place for the use of your own foreign mobile phone, but note these are designed not so much for your convenience as pay for the Telco CEOs latest marvellously facilitated ocean-going mega yacht.

Time difference
New Zealand Standard Time (NZST) is 12 hrs ahead of GMT. From the 1st Sun in Oct to the 3rd Sun in Mar the clock goes forward 1 hr.

Tipping
Tipping in New Zealand is at the customer's discretion. In a good restaurant you should leave a tip of 10-15% if you are satisfied with the service, but the bill may include a service charge. Tipping is appreciated in pubs and bars and taxi drivers also expect some sort of tip; on a longer journey 10% is fine. As in most other countries, hotel porters, bellboys, waiters and waitresses should all be tipped to supplement their meager wages.

Tourist information
The official New Zealand Visitor Information Network is made up of around 100 accredited Visitor Information Centres (VICs) nationally known as i-SITES. Familiarize yourself with the green and black silver fern logo upon arrival.

National i-SITES are based in Auckland and Christchurch as well as the main tourist centres, like Rotorua and Queenstown. Open 7 days a week, they provide a comprehensive information service including accommodation bookings and domestic airline, bus and train ticketing. Souvenir shops and occasionally other retail outlets, currency exchange and cafés are often attached.

Regional i-SITES are found throughout the country and there may be more than one in each region. They provide a general information booking service usually 7 days a week and there is also a huge amount of free material.

Local i-SITES can be found almost anywhere, providing local information as well as assistance in accommodation and transport bookings. They are open at least 5 days a week, but are subject to varying seasonal and weekend hours. For detail refer newzealand.com/travel/i-sites.

Useful websites
For general information start with purenz.com, the official website of the New Zealand Tourism Board. Others include destination-nz.com, searchnz.co.nz and tourism.net.nz. The Department of Conservation website doc.govt.nz provides detailed information on national parks and tramping tracks. For weather, refer to metservice.co.nz and the forecast charts metvuw.com. For New Zealand imagery refer to the author's website darrochdonaldnz.com.

Contents

Footprint features

Canterbury & the West Coast

Christchurch and Banks Peninsula

Dubbed the Garden City, Christchurch is known as being the most English of New Zealand's cities. Reminders of these roots are everywhere from the formal blazers and straw hats of the city's school children to the distant chorus of 'howzat' from its myriad cricket pitches on lazy summer Sunday afternoons. Without doubt the key to its charm is the immense, tree-lined Hagley Park that borders its centre and has over the decades remained largely intact, even after the 2011 earthquake. With the park, its trees and the pretty Avon River that threads it all together, the aesthetics of Christchurch verge on the adorable. But natural aesthetics and its obvious English colonial feel aside, Christchurch has developed its own very Kiwi-orientated atmosphere. It has the buzz and vitality of Auckland, the cosmopolitan town feel of Wellington and it shares a pride in its heritage and architecture that only Dunedin can beat.

In 1850 the 'first four ships' (as they became known) – the *Charlotte Jane*, *Randolph*, *Sir George Seymour* and *Cressy* brought 782 colonial souls to the then whaling base of Lyttleton, which had already been established on the Banks Peninsula. Even before their arrival, the Canterbury Association (formed in Britain in 1849) had already christened the great settlement-to-be, Christchurch.

Arriving in Christchurch

Getting there
Air Christchurch International Airport ① *T03-3585029, christchurch-airport.co.nz*, is 12 km northwest of the city via Fendalton Road and Memorial Avenue. **Metro buses** ① *T03-3668855, metro info.org.nz*, offer a regular Red Bus City Flyer service to the CBD and Cathedral Square (hourly Monday-Friday 0600-2300, Saturday/Sunday 0800-2300, $7.50) (No 29, 20 minutes). Various shuttles, including **Super Shuttle** (door to door) ① *T03-3579950, T0800-SHUTTLE*. A taxi from the airport costs around $40, **Blue Star** ① *T03-3531200, T03-3799799, 24 hrs*, or **First Direct** ① *T03-3775555*.

Bus Regional and national buses arrive and depart from either Cathedral Square in Christchurch, or at the **Christchurch Travel Centre** ① *123 Worcester Blvd, T03-377 0951*.

Train Christchurch's train station is on Addington Street, 3 km from the city centre at the southwestern tip of Hagley Park.

Tourist information
i-SITE visitor centre ① *Old Post Office Building, Cathedral Sq (West), T03-379 9629, christchurchnz.com, christchurchinformation.co.nz, localeye.co.nz, Mon-Fri 0830-1700, Sat-Sun 0830-1600*. There are also i-SITES in the international (T03-353 7783/4) and domestic (T03-353 7774/5) airport terminals.

Places in Christchurch

Cathedral Square
Prior to the 2011 earthquake (and as the name suggests) the square was dominated by the 63-m spire of the 1881 Gothic-revival Anglican **Christ Church Cathedral**. Infamously, the spire collapsed during the earthquake and initially there were fears that up to 20 people had been buried in the rubble. Thankfully however no-one died at the site. But the collapse of the spire, which was caught on a mobile phone, quickly became the defining footage of the devastation and for many a representation of the assault on the city's heart and soul.

Although the future of both the cathedral and the site (which was deconsecrated in October 2011) remains uncertain, planning is underway for a complete rebuild. In the interim, plans for a transitional cathedral designed by renowned international architect Shigeru Ban have been adopted. It is hoped that this inspirational building dubbed the 'Cardboard Cathedral' will open in time for Christmas 2012. The square is also home to the statue of John Robert Godley the founder of the Canterbury Association and essentially Christchurch itself and the Four Ships Court, a memorial to the 'first four ships' that stands outside the 1879 Old Post Office. The Old Post Office used to house the **Visitor Information Centre** ① *T03-379 9629, christchurchnz.com*, which is now located beside the Canterbury Museum (Botanic Gardens) on Rolleston Avenue.

Avon River
Though hardly the Mississippi this little river is without doubt one of the city's greatest assets. Meandering from the northwest tip of the four avenues through Hagley Park and the Botanical Gardens, it cuts furtively through the city centre, before finally continuing its journey through the city's eastern suburbs to the sea. The river is particularly attractive

The Christchurch earthquake of 2011

New Zealand is often referred to as the 'Shakey Isles' and owes many of its natural features – indeed, its very existence – to the fact that it lies on a series of fault lines associated with the interactions of major tectonic plates. Subsequently, volcanic activity and earthquakes are a fundamental part of its natural and human history.

But, if there were one place you would have left off the list of places most susceptible it would be Christchurch. The city was not thought to be lying directly over any major fault lines and had no history of major earthquakes throughout its short human history.

A 7.1-magnitude 'quake in late 2010 was certainly alarming and caused significant damage in the city but, for the vast majority, it caused little more than a raised eyebrow and a brief shelf rearrangement. Then, six months later, at 12.51 pm on 22 February 2011, it struck – and this time it was local. At a magnitude of 6.3 it was not as powerful as the 2010 'quake in central Canterbury, but the combination of its location, timing and the intensity of the ground shaking (which was among the strongest ever recorded in an urban area) proved catastrophic. In total 185 people lost their lives and much of the city centre infrastructure was destroyed or damaged beyond repair. Amid the many aftershocks that lasted well in to 2012 it seemed the very heart and soul of Christchurch had been destroyed.

Cantabrians, however, are stoic and the city is steadily recovering. Despite the damage and the transition it still has plenty to offer the visitor and it should remain on any South Island itinerary.

in autumn when poplar and weeping willows are radiant in golden hues. On the eastern bank of the river, just beyond Cathedral Square is the 1917 statue of Scott of the Antarctic beside the river – a reminder that Christchurch is a principal gateway to the Antarctic.

Beside the Worcester Boulevard Bridge and at the 1882 **Antigua Boat Sheds** ① *2 Cambridge Terr, T03-366 0337, punting.co.nz, daily 0900-2100, winter 1000-1600, 30 mins, $25, child $12*, you will find bases for punting, a congenial mode of river transport that hails from the university towns of Oxford and Cambridge in the UK.

Located 3.5 km west of the city centre on the banks of the Avon are **Riccarton Bush** and **Riccarton House (Putaringamotu)** ① *16 Kahu Rd, T03-341 1018, riccartonhouse.co.nz*. Set in 12 ha of parkland, the historic Riccarton Estate was once the home of the Scots pioneers and brothers William and John Deans (the first European settlers on the Canterbury Plains). It features the faithfully restored and furnished original 1843 **Deans cottage** ① *open daily*, in which they first lived, and the grand Victorian/Edwardian **homestead** ① *Mon-Fri 1300-1600*, that was built by the next generation from 1856 to 1874. Although the homestead may still be closed due to the earthquake, the cottage and grounds remain open.

Hagley Park
① *T03-941 7590. Daily Sep-Apr Mon-Fri 0900-1600, Sat-Sun 1000-1400.*
Amazingly intact after all the years of development and largely unaffected by the earthquake, Hagley Park (over 200 ha) is divided in two portions by Riccarton Avenue and comprises pleasant tree-lined walkways, sports fields and, in its central reaches, the **Botanical Gardens** ① *0700-dusk, Conservatory Complex 1015-1600*, enclosed by a loop of the Avon River. Well maintained and with a huge variety of gardens from herb to rose,

these provide a great escape from the buzz of the city year round. Autumn sees the gardens at their most colourful. There is an information centre and café housed in old Curators House off Rolleston Avenue.

Arts centres
Two entities along Worcester Boulevard, one old and one new, once dominated the arts scene in the city.

The **Christchurch Art Gallery (Te Puna O Waiwhetu)** ① *T03-941 7300, christchurchart gallery.org.nz, daily 1000-1700, Wed 2100, free with a charge for major exhibitions*, was upon its completion in 2003 immediately christened by some cynics as 'a warehouse in a tutu'. It is actually supposed to be 'evoking the sinuous form of the koru and the River Avon that flows through Christchurch', but whether you love it or frown at it with over 3000 sq m of exhibition space, it can certainly accommodate a formidable 5500 permanent works. Significantly damaged in the earthquake it is due to be reopened in mid-2013. Beyond its almost mesmerizingly colourful 'grand stair' you will find a dynamic range of contemporary exhibitions and an many of the famous New Zealand names including Charles Goldie, Colin McCahon and Ralph Hotere. There is also a retail outlet and the obligatory café/bistro.

The more historic Gothic Revival buildings along Worcester Boulevard was once the site of the original University of Canterbury and then the popular Christchurch Arts Centre.

Christchurch

To **1 5**, Kaikoura, Airport, SH1 North, Antarctic Centre, Orana Park & Willowbank Reserve

Where to stay 🛏
Airport Christchurch
  Motel **1** *A2*
Orari Bed & Breakfast **2** *B2*
Chester Street
  Backpackers **3** *B3*

George **4** *B2*
Meadow Park Top
Ten Holiday Park **5** *A2*

Restaurants 🍴
50 Bistro & Bar **1** *B2*

Himalayas **2** *B2*
Pescatore **3** *B2*
Vic's Café & Bakehouse **4** *A2*

500 metres
500 yards

Functioning as the Arts Centre it housed an excellent and dynamic array of arts and crafts, workshops, galleries and sales outlets, as well as theatres, cinemas, cafés, restaurants and bars. But sadly, on 22 February 2011, almost all that eclectic activity ceased and given the damage it remains closed indefinitely. One exception is the **Canterbury Cheesemongers** ① *301 Montreal St, T03-379 0075, Tue-Fri 0900-1700, Sat 1000-1600,* housed in the more modern Registry Building. As well as selling a fine range of regionally produced cheeses it sells its own baked breads and operates as a café.

Canterbury Museum and Christ College
① *Rolleston Av, T03-366 5000 cantmus.govt.nz. Daily 0900-1730 (winter 1700), entry is free but there are small charges for the Exhibition Court and Discovery Centre ($2); guided tours also available on Tue and Thu at 1530-1630.*

Housed in a grand 1870 neo-Gothic building and founded in 1867, the region's largest museum is well worth a visit and has reopened despite the earthquake. Other than the new and obvious exhibition surrounding the earthquake itself highlights include its impressive Maori collection and the Hall of Antarctic Discovery. In keeping with other museums in the country, it also hosts a dynamic Discovery Centre for kids. The Exhibition Court displays a changing programme of travelling national and international exhibitions. There is also a fine in-house shop and a café overlooking the Botanical Gardens.

Just north of the museum is **Christ College Canterbury**, which is without doubt New Zealand's most famous historic school. Built in 1850 it is an aesthetic and architectural delight, and in the late afternoon spills forth suitably clad and 'proper' scholars.

International Antarctic Centre
① *38 Orchard Rd (near the airport, signposted), T03-353 7798, iceberg.co.nz. Daily Oct-Mar 0900-1900, Apr-Sep 0900-1730; $35, child $20 for entry and Penguin Encounter; $65, child $35 provides unlimited entry all day to the NZ Penguin Encounter Hagglund Ride and 4D Extreme Theatre. Guided tours are available or you can self-guide with the help of 'snow-phones' ($6). There is a free Penguin Express bus from the VIC on the corner of Montreal and Worcester Blvd, on the hour from 1000-1600.*

Since the days of Scott and Shackleton, Christchurch has been a principal 'gateway to the Antarctic'. Today, an area alongside the airport is a working campus to which a formidable array of buildings can attest. From here you can often see the US Hercules sitting waiting to head off into the wild blue and very cold yonder. The International Antarctic Centre is the public face of operations and was opened in 1992. Though somewhat pricey it offers an excellent introduction to the great white continent and overall it is both informative and fun, with an excellent array of displays from the historical to the modern day. Highlights include the **Snow and Ice Experience**, a room kept at -5°C, replete with manufactured snow and ice, and **Penguin Encounter**, comprising a small group of mainly rehabilitated and permanently disabled little blue penguins – a species that is, ironically, far more at home around the golden beaches of Australasia than the icebergs of Antarctica. From the 4D Extreme Theatre and static displays you then emerge into the well and unusually stocked Antarctic shop and the South Café and Bar – more likely for a stiff whiskey than a double-scoop ice cream.

In addition to the centre's indoor activities is the Antarctic Hagglund Ride. The Hagglund is a tracked vehicle that was originally used on the Scott and McMurdo bases. During the 15-minute ride you are taken to see some of the major facilities of the centre before experiencing the all-terrain abilities of the vehicle.

Lyttleton, the Gondola and Banks Peninsula views

If you are short of time the following half-day drive offers some memorable views of the city and the Banks Peninsula and gives you a far better sense of place than the flat milieu of the city and the plains that surround it.

From the city centre head southeast along Moorhouse, then Ferry Roads towards Sumner. Then take Tunnel Road (SH74) to Lyttleton. Once through the tunnel take some time to look around Lyttelton. **Lyttelton i-SITE visitor centre** ① *20 Oxford St, T03-328 9093, lytteltonharbour.co.nz, daily 0900-1700*, can provide detailed information and a self-guided historical-walks leaflet.

Although visiting cruise liners and container ships now mask Lyttleton Harbour's history, this was the place where the 'first four ships' arrived in 1850. It was also the port that Captain Scott and Lieutenant Shackleton used as their base to explore the Antarctic and is still regularly used by Antarctic service and tourist vessels. From Lyttleton head east around the hills on Sumner Road, then once you turn back inland head up left on Summit Road. Summit Road winds its way up and along the Port Hills offering great views across the city north and west. You can also access various viewpoints looking south over the peninsula including the Gondola complex.

Continue west along Summit Road until it drops to Dyers Pass Road. Before descending back in to the city it is worth taking in the view from Coronation Hill Reserve that overlooks the Cashmere Valley and Lyttelton Harbour. The curiously named building Sign of the Kiwi was opened in 1917 as a tearoom and inn and is one of a chain of similar buildings, built by local politician Henry Ell, in the early 1900s and used as staging posts along a hillside tourist route. The Sign of the Takahe a little further back towards the city is now a fine-dining restaurant. From there just follow your nose back in to the city centre.

Wildlife attractions

Christchurch has two main wildlife attractions both located near the airport.

Orana Park ① *743 McLeans Island Rd, 10 mins from the airport, T03-3597109, oranawildlifepark.co.nz, daily 1000-1700, from $25, child $8*, New Zealand's largest captive wildlife reserve, is set in 80 ha of parkland. It has native and international wildlife with an emphasis on African animals, including meerkats.

Willowbank Wildlife Reserve ① *60 Hussey Rd, off Gardiners Rd, T03-3596226, willowbank.co.nz, daily 1000-2200, $25, child $10*, focuses primarily on native wildlife and farm animals. The reserve has a successful kiwi-breeding programme and one of the better kiwi exhibits in the country. Weekends are best avoided, however, as it gets busy. The reserve is also base for the **KoTane Maori Experience** ① *daily at 1730, 1830 winter performance and Hangi (traditional Maori meal) only, $105, child $67.50; performance, Hangi and kiwi tour, $135, child $80*.

Christchurch (Port Hills) Gondola

① *10 Bridle Path Rd, T03-384 0700, gondola.co.nz*.

The Christchurch Gondola is worth the trip and although extensively damaged during the earthquake and subsequently closed for almost two years the centre has now reopened. The base terminal is in the Heathcote Valley 10 km southeast of the city via Ferry Road.

From there gondolas whisk you 945 m to the top of the Port Hills (1500 m) and the Summit Complex. The complex has all the expected shops and a café but also offers viewpoints from which you can gaze down to Lyttleton and across the Banks Peninsula, or beyond the Canterbury Plains, to the Southern Alps. You can embark on a number of walks from the complex including one that explores the crater rim.

Banks Peninsula
Jutting out into the Pacific Ocean from Christchurch is the Banks Peninsula. Captain Cook was the first European to discover the peninsula, but he actually thought it was an island (which it actually once was) and charted it as such, bestowing on it the name Banks Island after his ship's naturalist Sir Joseph Banks. Distinctly out of character with the (now) connected and flat alluvial Canterbury Plains, it is a refreshing and rugged landscape of hills and flooded harbours formed by two violent volcanic eruptions. The two largest harbours, which now fill the craters and shelter their namesake settlements, are **Lyttleton** to the north and **Akaroa** to the south. These settlements provide an interesting excursion from Christchurch, with Akaroa a long but scenic 85 km drive and Lyttleton – 12 km away via the Lyttleton Tunnel – being by far the more accessible.

Other than the hill and harbour scenery, both places offer historic sites, and activities such as dolphin watching. The bays and waters that surround the peninsula are home to the world's smallest and rarest dolphin, the Hector's dolphin. The two- or four-day trek on the Banks Peninsula Track from Akaroa is also a popular attraction.

The **Akaroa visitor centre** ① *80 Rue Lavaud, T03-304 8600, akaroa.com, daily 0900-1700,* is an independent information office, with helpful staff, who will share their knowledge regarding the village and more out-of-the-way places.

Christchurch and Banks Peninsula listings

For hotel and restaurant price codes and other relevant information, see pages 9-13.

⊜ Where to stay

Christchurch *p23, map p25*
$$$ Airport Christchurch Motel, 55 Roydvale Av, Christchurch, T03-9774970, T0800-800631, airportchristchurch.co.nz. Modern 4-star handy to the airport with self-contained options. Bealey Av on the way in from the airport has dozens of other motel options.
$$ The George Hotel, 50 Park Terr, T03-379 4560, thegeorge.com. Overlooking the river and handy for the Arts Centre, The George has a solid reputation with excellent, well-appointed suites, facilities and award-winning cuisine.
$$ Orari Bed and Breakfast, 42 Gloucester St, T0800 267274, T03-3656569, orari.net.nz.

Former heritage house, fully renovated with modern decor and in a convenient central location. 10 elegant suites and shared lounge with private entrance.
$ Chester Street Backpackers, 148 Chester St, T03-3771897, chesterst.co.nz. Classic, small 'home away from home' hostel. Cosy, with plenty of character and well facilitated. Double, twin and shared rooms and a fully self-contained cottage nearby. Recommended. Also affiliated with a reliable second-hand campervan dealership for those new arrivals hoping to hit the road.

Motor parks
$$$-$ Meadow Park Top Ten Holiday Park, 39 Meadow St (off Papanui Rd at the northwestern end of the city), T03-3529176, meadowpark.co.nz. Has a great range of options from self-contained motels, lodges and flats to chalets, cottages and standard

cabins, powered/tent sites. That said, you pay more for its location and the facilities, which include a spa pool, sauna and weight training room. Look out for the sign off Papanui Rd as it's hard to spot.

🍴 Restaurants

Christchurch *p23, map p25*
Pre earthquake Christchurch had some popular drinking and eating conglomerates, but being well within the CBD all that has now changed. New or relocated eateries are beginning to make their mark elsewhere and many find the transition exciting. Given the circumstances and the ad hoc nature of their location by far the best way to find the most worthwhile places is by word of mouth. Ask the locals or simply experiment.
$$$ Himalayas, 830 Colombo St, T03 3778935, himalayas.co.nz. Open lunch Tue-Fri 1130-1400, dinner Tue-Sun 1700-late. Pre earthquake there was a scattering of reliable Indian restaurants in the city and thankfully, now, Himalayas can hold the fort until others can re-establish – not that they might want them to! Takeaways are also available.
$$-$ The 50 Bistro and Bar & The Pescatore, 50 Park Terr, T03-371 0250, thegeorge.com. Both centrally located in the George Hotel and overlooking the river '50' enjoys a solid reputation for mid-budget, while the Pescatore, with its ultra uber interior design, offers award-winning à la carte.
$$-$ Vic's Café and Bakehouse, 132 Victoria St, T03 3662054, vics.co.nz. Open Mon-Fri 0700-1700, Sat and Sun 0730-1700. It's not just the famous nutty porridge that draws the locals here, or the quality breakfast/brunches. A fine cosmopolitan vibe, eclectic menu and adjunct bakery put this one firmly on the 'be back again' list.

🍸 Bars and clubs

Christchurch *p23, map p25*
Christchurch Casino, 30 Victoria St, T03-365 9999, chchcasino.co.nz. A well-established institution and naturally a popular entertainment venue.
Culture Club, 4 His Lordships Lane, Sol Sq, Christchurch. Popular 1980s dance bar with lots of Wham! Open from 2100 until very late Thu-Sat.

🎭 Entertainment

Christchurch *p23, map p25*
For performance and cinema listings consult *The Press* newspaper, stuff.co.nz/the-pres. The free leaflet, *The Package* available from the i-SITE is also useful, thepackage.co.nz.

Cinema
Hoyts, 392 Moorhouse Av (Old Train Station), T0508-446987.
Rialto, corner Moorhouse Av and Durham St, T03-3749404.

🎉 Festivals

Christchurch *p23, map p25*
Mid-Jan World Busker's Festival, worldbuskersfestival.com. A lively event attracting street performers and musicians from around the world.
Jul/Aug Christchurch Arts Festival, artsfestival.co.nz. Includes theatre, dance, classical and jazz concerts, cabaret and exhibitions of the visual arts.

🛍 Shopping

Christchurch *p23, map p25*
Toffs Recycled Clothing, 141 Gloucester St, just off Cathedral Sq. An innocuous-looking place that gives no indication of the marvels inside. The perfect place for shopaphobics with all manner of second-hand clothing and accessories, from snow chains

to – if you're lucky – an Armani business shirt and silk tie. The challenge: try going in there for less than 20 mins and coming out empty handed.

⚙ What to do

Christchurch p23, map p25
Tour operators
Adventure Canterbury, T0800-847455, adventurecanterbury.com. One of the main activity operators in Christchurch, offering a wide array of trips and activities including jet boating, horse trekking, fishing, farm visits, winery tours and day trips to Hanmer and Akaroa.
Black Cat Group Lyttelton and Akaroa, T03-328 9078, blackcat.co.nz. Offers an interesting array of catamaran cruises from Lyttelton and Hector's dolphin watching/ swimming cruises from Akaroa.
Mountain Bike Adventure Company, T03-377 5952, T0800-424534, cyclehire-tours.co.nz. Offers a trip that goes up the Port Hills via the gondola to then descend by bike, $60, plus tours from 3-5 days and hire from $35 per day.

⊖ Transport

Christchurch p23, map p25
For travel information and bookings contact the regional i-SITE visitor centres. See also Arriving in Christchurch, page 23.

Christchurch is 336 km south of Picton (Kaikoura 183 km) via SH1; and 579 km north of Invercargill (Dunedin 362 km, Timaru 163 km) on SH1. Queenstown is 486 km southwest via SH1/SH8, and Greymouth, 258 km via Arthur's Pass and SH73.

Bus
Intercity is the main bus company, T03-3651113, intercity.co.nz. Christchurch has an excellent local public bus system with a modern terminal, the Bus Exchange, corner of Lichfield and Colombo streets. For all bus information contact T03-3668855, metroinfo.org.nz, or **Red Buses** T0800-733287, redbus.co.nz. The Free Yellow Shuttle takes in a north-south route from the casino, through Cathedral Sq and down Colombo St and back, every 10-15 mins (Mon-Fri 0730-2230, Sat 0800-2230, Sun 1000-2000). It's worth jumping on to get your bearings. **Best Attractions Shuttle** T0800-484485, takes in the main city attractions including the Antarctic Centre and the Gondola, departing Cathedral Sq, daily 0900-1800. Various fares including entry.

Train
TranzScenic operates the northbound 'TranzCoastal' service (departs 0730; to Kaikoura-Blenheim-Picton); and the deservingly popular 'TranzAlpine' (departs 0815; to Greymouth), T0800-872467, tranzscenic.co.nz.

ⓘ Directory

Christchurch p23, map p25
ATM There are ATMs and currency exchange available at the airport and the i-SITE visitor centre. All the major banks are represented in the CBD.
Hospital Southern Cross Hospital, 131 Bealey Av, T03-9683100.
Pharmacy 555 or 748 Colombo St.

Around Christchurch

From Christchurch SH1 heads north and is embraced by the Hurunui hills. At Waipara, SH7 heads northeast to Hanmer Springs and the West Coast via the Lewis Pass, while SH1 continues north to Kaikoura and eventually Blenheim. In landlocked Hanmer activities include skiing, rafting, horse trekking and mountain biking. All these activities are in addition to the more obvious and soporific attraction of its hot pools in the thermal resort. Kaikoura, in contrast and almost miniaturized in the shadow of the Kaikoura mountain ranges, is equally abuzz with activity. But here the emphasis is most definitely on the colder waters of the ocean and its inhabitants. At Kaikoura you can view an impressive list of sea creatures including albatrosses, seals, dolphins and of course Kaikoura's very own whales.

If you're heading south from Christchurch, SH1 passes through the flat heartland of the Canterbury Plains to Timaru. With so much stunning scenery elsewhere in New Zealand, it is often labelled as the least exciting drive in the country; only the occasional glimpse of the distant Southern Alps far to the west and the odd wide pebble-strewn riverbed crossing, breaks the monotony of the endless roadside windbreaks and expansive fields.

North of Christchurch

Hanmer Springs

ⓘ *Amuri Av, T03-315 7511, T0800-442663, hanmersprings.co.nz. Daily 1000-2100, $18, child $9 (same-day return pass $23, child $12).*

The name derives from the name of Canterbury pioneer Thomas Hanmer who no doubt had a lifelong struggle with his 'M-n-Ns'. Hanmer has long been popular with Kiwi holiday-seekers, and is now a top national tourist venue. Its biggest attraction is of course its impressive **Thermal Reserve**, which is (arguably) the best in the country.

The springs were first discovered by the Europeans in 1859 and later became a commercial venture and public attraction; in 1907, the first facilities and a hotel formed the beginnings of the resort and, subsequently, the town as a whole. The resort has enjoyed an impressive expansion and improvement in recent years, and has various pools including open and landscaped, freshwater, swimming and a children's play pool – all connected by steaming boulder streams. The mineral-rich waters range in temperature from 30-47°C. Also on site are a massage and beauty clinic, private pools, saunas, a steam room, a licensed café and a picnic area.

Hanmer is also a very popular base for mountain biking and walking in the Hanmer Forest Park. The town offers a wide range of modern accommodation, some good restaurants and numerous other activities from bungee jumping to horse trekking and is particularly beautiful in autumn when the forest and tree-lined streets are flush with golden hues and falling leaves.

For detailed information call in at the **Hanmer Springs i-SITE visitor centre** ⓘ *next to the thermal reserve, 42 Amuri Av, T03-3150020, T0800-442663, visithanmersprings.co.nz.*

Lewis Pass

From Hanmer Springs SH7 crosses the northern ranges of the Great Divide (Southern Alps) to the west coast via the Lewis Pass (864 m), Maruia Springs (another smaller thermal springs resort), Springs Junction and the former mining town of Reefton (130 km).

The name Lewis derives from Henry Lewis (surveyor) who came across it in the early 1860s but well before that the Ngai Tahu Maori of Canterbury used this route to access the west coast in search of pounamu (greenstone). Having negotiated the pass on their return, they are said to have dispensed with their slaves – alas not with a 'thanks lads, see you next year', but a brutal death followed by a feast of their various bodily parts. Alas, perhaps right there and then corporations and capitalism were created!

Although not as dramatic as Arthur's Pass (see overleaf) further to the south the Lewis offers some lovely scenery and a few good walking opportunities along the way. It also boasts a mountain with one of the most unusual names in the country. There are many with wonderful names, but frankly 'Mons Sex Millia' has to take the biscuit. Of course the translation is a real balloon burster; it actually means 'six peaky bits' – or words to that effect!

Kaikoura → *See map, page 34.*

Kaikoura is aesthetically stunning and is also home to a wealth of sea creatures. For the wildlife enthusiast the Kaikoura Coast is on a par with the Otago Peninsula for richness and accessibility to some of New Zealand's biggest and most famous wildlife icons. This is due to the topography and depth of the ocean floor: just south of Kaikoura, a trough comes unusually close to the coastline creating an upsurge of nutritious plankton soup, giving rise to the many creatures with which we are more familiar further up the food chain. At the very top of course is the majestic and much-victimized king of them all – the whale. But here you can also get up close and personal with many others including dolphins, seals and those mighty masters of flight – albatrosses.

Prior to your arrival consider what you want to see and how. You can see whales by boat or from the air, you can swim with dolphins and seals, go diving, kayaking or fishing. But a word of warning; factor in an extra day in case of inclement weather. Like the West Coast it can be very frustrating imagining yourself partaking in all these great activities only to end up in a café watching rain drops in street puddles. Also, in the high season you will need to book whale watching or dolphin swimming in advance, see page 40.

The **Kaikoura i-SITE visitor centre** ① *West End, T03-319 5641, kaikoura.co.nz*, can provide non-biased detail on the full range of options.

Arthur's Pass

The **Arthur's Pass visitor information centre (DoC)** ① *T03-318 9211, doc.govt.nz, daily 0900-1600*, is in the heart of the village on the southern side of SH73. It has various displays about the national park, a video ($1), walks information and all local accommodation and service details. But before embarking on any long walks or tramps check the weather forecast and ask about up to date track conditions.

The route (258 km) to Greymouth and the west coast via SH73 from Christchurch across the Great Divide and the northern ranges of the Southern Alps is one of the most celebrated scenic drives and rail journeys in the country. It is most notable perhaps for its sheer range of dramatic South Island landscapes from the flatlands of the Canterbury Plains to the east, through the rugged mountain peaks and braided rivers in its centre, to the lush coastal valleys and lakes to the west. On the way the Craigieburn Forest and Arthur's Pass National Parks offer some excellent walking, tramping, rock climbing and skiing opportunities.

Arthur Dudley Dobson, a pioneer surveyor, was the first to explore the route in 1864. Due to the gold boom a basic road was built within a year of his observations, but the rail link that later served the coal and timber trade took a further 60 years to complete.

South of Christchurch

Timaru
① *Timaru i-SITE visitor centre, 2 George St, T03-688 6163, southisland.org.nz/timaru.asp.*
The port city of Timaru, halfway between Christchurch and Dunedin, provides a refreshing stopover on SH1, or a convenient starting point from which to head west, via SH8, to the MacKenzie Country, Mount Cook and Queenstown. The city is pleasant, boasting the popular Caroline Bay beach near the town centre, a few good parks, the region's main museum, a reputable art gallery and a few unique attractions, including some ancient seventh-century Maori rock art.

The South Canterbury Museum
① *Perth St, T03-684 2212, Tue-Fri 1000-1630, Sat-Sun 1330-1630, free.*
The main regional museum and contains some interesting exhibits on local maritime history, Maori rock art and the exploits of local farmer and wannabe aviator Richard Pearse (1877-1953). In April 1903, at the tender age of 26, Pearse created history by making the first-ever powered flight in a 'heavier-than-air-man-carrying aeroplane'. His flight, though neither long nor spectacular, was a world first and was completed nine months before the better-

Kaikoura

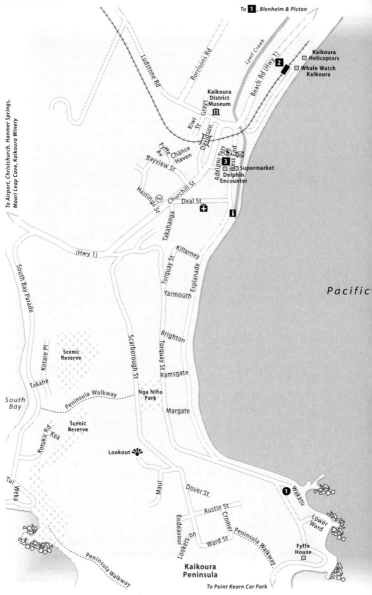

To **1**, Blenheim & Picton

Kaikoura Helicopters
Whale Watch Kaikoura
Beach Rd (Hwy 1)
Lyell Creek

Ludstone Rd
Rorrisons Rd

Grays
Kiwi St
Davidson
Kaikoura District Museum

Fyffe Chance Av Haven
Bayview St

3
Supermarket
Dolphin Encounter
Adelphi Ter

Hastings St
Churchill St
Deal St
1

Takahanga
(Hwy 1)
Killarney
Torquay St
Esplanade
Yarmouth

Brighton
Torquay St
Ramsgate

Scarborough St
Nga Niho Park
Margate

To Airport, Christchurch, Hanmer Springs, Maori Leap Cave, Kaikoura Winery

South Bay Parade

Kotare Pl
Takahe
Scenic Reserve
Peninsula Walkway

South Bay
Scenic Reserve
Koruku Rd
Kea

Tui
Weka
Lookout

Maui
Dover St

Endeavour
Austin St
Cromel St
Lookerson
Ward St

1 Wakatu
Lower Ward
Peninsula Walkway

Fyffe House

Peninsula Walkway

Kaikoura Peninsula

To Point Kearn Car Park

Pacific

known and much-celebrated flight by the American pioneer aviator Orville Wright of the famous Wright brothers. However, unlike the celebrated Wright brothers, Pearse died an unrecognized recluse in a psychiatric hospital in Christchurch. A full replica of his impressive flying machine is on display in the museum. Other relics of Pearse's flying inventions are held at the **Pleasant Point Railway Museum** ① *18 km northwest of Timaru (SH8), T03-6862269, pleasantpointrail.org.nz.*

MacKenzie Country

The area known as the MacKenzie Country refers mainly to the flat expanse of tussock grasslands that make up the watersheds of the Tekapo and Gray rivers beyond Fairlie and south to Omarama. It is a strange barren landscape, devoid of trees and almost analogous to the plains of heartland USA. There is nowhere else like it in New Zealand and it bears little semblance to the lofty peaks that rise from around its edge. The name MacKenzie was bestowed upon it through the almost legendary sheep rustling activities of Scottish pioneer James 'Jock' MacKenzie.

Lake Tekapo

In the heart of MacKenzie Country is Lake Tekapo, a pretty little place, famous for its lakeside church and an ever-watchful little collie dog. However, over the last five years or so Tekapo has suffered somewhat from the rapacious development so evident throughout the central South Island and spreading north from Queenstown. Already parts of the village are looking horribly like a Christchurch suburb and it seems 'the money' has arrived, which is enough to have the little collie heading for the hills with its tail between its legs.

Just about everybody who visits Lake Tekapo pays homage to the **Church of the Good Shepherd**, which sits alone, in a picture-postcard position overlooking the lake. Built in 1935 it remains a functional

200 metres
200 yards

Where to stay 🛏
Hapuku Lodge **1**
Kaikoura Top Ten
 Holiday Park **2**
Lemon Tree Lodge **3**

Restaurants 🍴
Pier Hotel Pub & Café **1**

Mount Sunday and the Rangitata River Valley

Until recently there were basically two main reasons tourists headed for the hills west of Christchurch. The most obvious reason was to reach the west coast via SH73 and Arthur's Pass, while the other was to ski the popular Mount Hutt ski fields near Methven. However, since the release of the *Lord of the Rings* trilogy, there is now another very good reason in the surprising form of a large and conspicuous lump of rock. Mount Sunday, which sits predominantly in the Rangitata River Valley and in stark contrast against the mountainous skyline of Southern Alps, became the perfect filming location and set for Edoras and Meduseld, King Theoden's grand hall in the realm of Rohan. Although the set is long gone, it remains one of the most scenic drives in the region and, even without all the hype, was always a great place to visit. There are organized tours available from Christchurch (see page 40) or you can go it alone. Ask at the Christchurch i-SITE visitor centres for detailed directions.

place of worship, but sadly its modern-day function is almost entirely aesthetic, and the minister, who is in attendance almost daily, must tend a very superficial and transitory flock (the vast majority of whom fall out of tour buses and come only to worship the Lord Digital, Kodak and Text SMS). Whatever you do, go early in the morning or late in the day to avoid the hordes.

A few pew lengths from the church is a statue of a collie sheepdog; a simple tribute to the shepherd's best friend.

If you have time (and a rugged vehicle) the unsealed roads on either side of Lake Tekapo are well worth exploring. The road to the west passes Lake Alexandria and Lake McGregor both of which are very peaceful (and full of trout), before winding its way north to terminate at the Godley Peak Station.

Dominating the scene at the western end of Tekapo Village is **Mount John**, which at 300 m offers great views and a suitable home for the University of Canterbury's Astronomical Observatory. Open to the public its popular **Earth and Sky** ① *T03-680 6960, earthandsky.co.nz; day tours 1200-1500, 40 mins from $50, child $25; night tours, 2 hrs from $105, child $60; café open 1000-1700*, offers daytime guided tours and night stargazing. Weather permitting, the stargazing tour is fascinating and offers a great opportunity to see such heavenly bodies as the Alpha-Centuri, Southern Cross, Scorpius and, if you're really lucky, Kylieminorearendi. Even if you cannot join the tours the café is well worth a visit for the views.

Back down to earth and at the base of Mount John is Tekapo's latest attraction the **Alpine Springs, Spa & Winter Park** ① *6 Lakeside Dr, T03-680 6550, T0800 23538283, alpinesprings.co.nz, open daily 1000-2100; hot pools from $20, child $11; ice-skating $16, child $12; snow tubing $20, child $16; combo deals available*. The facility offers three hot pools and several private hot tubs that look out over the lake and range in temperature from 36-40°C. The day spa offers the standard facilities and treatments including sauna, steam room and massage. The Winter Park comprises an ice rink for skating, ice hockey and curling events and outside a snow-tubing run, in effect a 100-m-long artificial snow slope with purpose-built contours for snow tubing.

Mount Cook National Park

Some 50 km south of Lake Tekapo and 8 km north of Twizel, the famed SH80 skirts the western banks and azure waters of **Lake Pukaki** to pay homage to Aoraki (Mount Cook). Before entering the chancel you are first advised to admire the cathedral from afar from the southern banks of the lake. There is a car park, information centre and lookout point from which, on a clear day, the mountain beckons. Unless you are really pressed for time, or the weather is foul, it really is sacrilege not to make the scenic 55-km drive to **Mount Cook Village**. Located so close to the base of the mountains and **Hooker and Tasman Glacier** valleys, it is like a miniature toy-town which acts as the gateway to national park. This 70,696-ha park has to be one of the most spectacular in New Zealand, and the scenery is second only to Milford Sound. With the 3754-m peak of **Mount Cook** as its altar, its robust ministers include Tasman (3498 m) and Mount Sefton (3158 m), surrounded by a supportive choir of 19 peaks all over 3000 m. Rising up to this great chancel are the vast and impressive Hooker and Tasman glaciers, which not only created the long nave but once blocked the very porch. All this natural architecture makes for world-class scenery and mountaineering. Indeed, it was here that Sir Edmund Hillary first started a career that was to reach its 'peak' on the summit of Everest in 1953. And once here, it seems a terrible waste not to explore the park from even closer quarters.

Glentanner Park ① *T03-4351855, glentanner.co.nz*, 32 km towards the mountain serves as a motor park and scenic flight-seeing base. If the weather is fine you are advised to stop here and consider the scenic flights and other activities on offer, perhaps over a coffee, in its café overlooking the mountain. Note other fixed-wing flight-seeing options are available from the Mount Cook airport 7 km east of the village (see below). If you are in a motorhome and intend to stay in the valley overnight, Glentanner can be home – there is good basic DoC campsite in Mount Cook Village but no fully facilitated motor park.

Upon arrival in Mount Cook Village (a further 23 km) you will be immediately struck at how ordered and dull in colour it is. This is not an accident, since the settlement comes within the boundary of the park and is therefore strictly controlled. The only real exception to this is the **Hermitage Hotel**, which many claim to be the most famous in New Zealand (while others hail it merely as a blot on the landscape).

There are a wide range of activities on offer that focus mainly on the Hooker and Tasman Glacier valleys and lakes, from short and multi-day walks/tramps, to kayaking and mountain biking. The airport (7 km) also serves as base for Mount Cook Ski Planes, a superb flight-seeing option that offers the exciting prospect of a snow-landing high up amidst the peaks on the Tasman Glacier.

Another great (and cheaper) option is the overnight tramp to the **Mueller Hut** which sits in an idyllic position (1768 m) on the ridge of Mount Oliver (1933 m) behind Mount Cook Village. Although a strenuous climb requiring a fair level of fitness, proper planning and equipment, it is a classic excursion. If you stay overnight in the Hut, the views at sunset and sunrise over the Hooker and Mount Cook especially are simply world class. In total it is a stiff four-hour climb each way. A further one-hour return will see you at the top of Mount Oliver, which, rumour has it, was the first peak in the region that Sir Edmund Hillary climbed.

For more park information, hut bookings, all activities and accommodation options within in the park visit the **DoC visitor centre** ① *just below the Hermitage, Larch Grove, T03-4351186, mtcooknz.com, daily 0830-1800; winter 0830-1700.* For comprehensive regional information the **Lake Pukaki Visitor Centre** ① *SH8, T03-4353280, mtcooknz.com, open daily 0900-1800*, can also assist.

Twizel

The town of Twizel was purpose-built in the 1960s to provide a home for workers involved with the Waitaki power scheme. Today, though a little soulless perhaps, it is a well-placed base for a host of activities mountain climbing, kayaking, mountain biking, skiing, horse trekking and hiking. It's also a place to see one of the rarest wading birds in the world – the Khaki, or **Black Stilt**. Thanks primarily to man's introduction of non-native predatory species, like the weasel and stoat, numbers have been decimated and currently total less than 100 wild birds. A **guided visit** ① *late Oct-mid Apr (weekdays only in winter), 0930 and 1630, $12.50, child $5; contact Twizel DoC, Wairepo Rd, Twizel, T03-4350802, doc.govt.nz*, to the viewing hide 3 km south of the village is available through DoC.

For comprehensive information on activities contact the **Twizel visitor information centre** ① *Market Pl, T03-4353124, twizel.com, daily Oct-Apr 0900-1800; May-Sep 1000-1600*.

Omarama

Located at the head of the Waitaki Valley (from Oamaru) and north of the scenic Lindis Pass (from Wanaka and Queenstown), Omarama provides a convenient overnight stop and finishing (or starting) point from which to explore the MacKenzie Country. There are a number of local activities that may detain you, including fishing and water sports on lakes Benmore, Aviemore and Ohau. Omarama is also world renowned for gliding. Other than the obvious appeal of the local lakes, the **Clay Cliffs** between Omarama and Twizel are worthy of investigation, and echo the bizarre eroded rock and gravel formations of the Pinnacles in the Wairarapa, North Island. To reach them turn off SH8 west towards the mountains on Quailburn Road, 3 km north of the village (signposted), 15 km. There is a small charge ($6) at the gate to the cliffs.

Around Christchurch listings

For hotel and restaurant price codes and other relevant information, see pages 9-13.

◯ Where to stay

Hanmer Springs *p32*
$$$$-$$$ Heritage Hotel and Resort,
1 Conical Hill Rd, T03-315 0060,
heritagehotels.co.nz. Modern and located overlooking the town centre. Rooms range from the honeymoon suite to standard, with self-contained standalone villas also available. It has all the usual facilities including a good restaurant, bar and a swimming pool. 2 mins from the hot pools.

Motor parks
$$-$ Alpine Adventure Tourist Park,
200 Jacks Pass Rd, south of the thermal resort, T03-3157112, aatouristpark.co.nz. A good walk from the town centre but

nonetheless an excellent choice with peaceful and spacious sheltered sites, excellent value cabins and good facilities.

Kaikoura *p32, map p34*
$$$$ Hapuku Lodge and Tree Houses,
Hapuku Rd (12 km north of Kaikoura),
T03-319 6559, hapukulodge.com.
A contemporary complex offering 7 elegant luxury en suites and an apartment with open fire and spa and the even more popular luxury 'Tree Houses' sleeping up to 5. The emphasis is very much on natural materials and a scattering of original New Zealand art. There is also a guest restaurant.
$$$ Lemon Tree Lodge, 31 Adelphi Terr,
T03-3197464, lemontree.co.nz. A boutique B&B that caters especially for couples or single independent travellers. Renovated 2-storey house with 4 tidy rooms, all with private deck or balcony and good attention

to detail. Outdoor hot tub. Caring and well-travelled owners.

Motor parks
$$$-$ Kaikoura Top Ten Holiday Park, 34 Beach Rd, T03-319 5362, T0800-363638, kaikouratop10.co.nz. The best motor park, only 3 mins from the town centre and the beach. Modern facilities, motel units, en suite units, cabins and powered/tent sites.

Lake Tekapo *p35*
$$$ Chalet Boutique Motel, 14 Pioneer Dr, T03-680 6774, thechalet.co.nz. A fine lodge-style motel. By the lake (near the church) with 6 tidy apartments and plenty of activities on offer.

Motor parks
$$-$ Lake Tekapo Motels and Motor Camp, Western end of the village close to Springs and Winter Park, Lakeside Dr, T03-680 6825, T0800-853853. Spacious and peaceful in a fine lakeside spot. Self-contained motels, flats, cabins and sheltered powered/tent sites, camp kitchen.

Mount Cook National Park *p37*
$$$$-$$$ Hermitage Hotel, Mount Cook Village, T03-435 1809, mount-cook.com. Iconic with standard rooms or self-contained motel doubles, studios and chalets with basic facilities. Bear in mind that the price reflects the location but there is no faulting the hotel facilities, and the restaurants and bars are good.

Motor parks
$$$-$ Glentanner Park and Activity Centre, SH80, 15 mins before Mt Cook, T03-435 1855, glentanner.co.nz. Glentanner Park is the only motor park in the valley, and the base for several fixed-wing and helicopter scenic flight operators. Good facilities.

Hanmer Springs *p32*
$$$-$$ Malabar, Alpine Pacific Centre, 5 Conical Hill Rd, T03-315 7745. Daily from 1800. A fine mix of Indian and Malaysian in a casual setting. Takeaway service.
$$ Alpine Village Inn, Jack's Pass Rd, T03-315 7005. Mon-Fri 1100-2130, Sat-Sun 0900-2130. Considered the local pub. Hearty, value pub food and relaxed friendly atmosphere.

Kaikoura *p32, map p34*
$$ Donegal House, Schoolhouse Rd (6 km via SH1 north), T03-319 5083. Daily 1100-1400 and 1800-2100. A good all rounder in a lovely rural setting. Small, atmospheric Irish country hotel/pub/restaurant with a mainly seafood menu including green-lipped mussels and local crayfish.
$$ Pier Hotel Pub and Café, 1 Avoca St, T03-319 5037. Daily from 1700. Combine a coastal walk to the wharf (1 km) with good pub-style grub, a fine atmosphere and views. Indoor and outdoor seating.

Lake Tekapo *p35*
$$ Astro Café, Mt John Observatory, Tekapo (follow signs west end of the village). Daily 0900-1700. Set atop the 300-m Mount John. Once you have taken in the lakeside views this is another excellent venue. Good coffee and standard café fare.

Mount Cook National Park *p37*
$$ Old Mountaineers Café Bar, just below the DoC visitor centre, Mount Cook Village, T03-435 1890. Daily for lunch and dinner. A fine alternative to the Hermitage Hotel Restaurants, offering a wholesome menu. It has a congenial atmosphere with open fire.

Omarama *p38*
$$ Clay Cliffs Vineyard and Café, 500 m south of Omarama on SH8, T03-438 9654, claycliffs.co.nz. Daily for lunch and dinner from 1100 (closed Jul). Tuscan-styled

restaurant with al fresco dining in a lovely relaxing setting. Try the local salmon.

❶ What to do

Hanmer Springs *p32*
Adventure activities
Hanmer Springs Adventure Centre (HSAC), 20 Conical Hill Rd, T03-315 7233, hanmeradventure.co.nz. Wide range of activities. Hire of mountain bikes, scooters, motorbikes (ATV adventures from $89), fishing tackle, rollerblades and ski equipment, also available.

Horse riding
Alpine Horse Safaris, Hawarden, T03-314 4293, alpinehorse.co.nz. Standard treks and some multi-day trips from $155.

Kaikoura *p32, map p34*
Tour operators
Dolphin and Albatross Encounter, 96 The Esplanade, T03-319 6777, T0800-733365, dolphin.co.nz. The main operator offering 3-hr trips from West End at 0530, 0830 and 1230, from $150, child $140 (viewing-only $80, child $40). Albatross and seabird trips from $110, child $55.
Glenstrae Farm 4 Wheeler Adventures, T03-319 7021, T0800-004009, 4wheeladventures.co.nz. 4WD and quad-bike adventures. Based about 25 km south of the town it offers 3-hr trips in the coastal hinterland, from $110. Courtesy pick-ups from Kaikoura.
Seal Swim Kaikoura, T03-3196182, T0800-732579, sealswimkaikoura.co.nz. 2-hr shore- and boat-based snorkeling tours from $70.
Whale Watch Kaikoura, T03-319 6767, T0800-655121, whalewatch.co.nz. Based at the Whaleway Station (next to the Railway Station), accessed off Beach Rd (SH1) just beyond West End. It offers several 2- to 3½-hr trips daily from $140, child $60.
Wings Over Whales, Peketa Airfield (6 km south of Kaikoura), T03-319 6580, T0800-226629, whales.co.nz. Entertaining and

personable flight-seeing trips 30-45 mins from $145, child $75.

Lake Tekapo *p35*
Tour operators
Air Safaris, Main St, T0800-806880, airsafaris.co.nz. The 'Grand Traverse' is a 50-min (200-km) trip that takes in Mt Cook and the glaciers. $280, child $195.

Mount Cook National Park *p37*
Kayaking
Glacier Sea-Kayaking, T03-4351890, mtcook.com. Explore the terminal face of the Tasman Glacier by kayak.

Tour operators
Glacier Explorers, T03-435 1641, T0800-686 800, glacierexplorers.com. Explore the terminal face of the Tasman Glacier by boat.
Helicopter Line, T03-435 1801, helicopter.co.nz. Its Mount Cook (East) operations are based at Glentanner park, 20-45 mins, from $200-$400.
Mount Cook Ski Planes, Mount Cook Airport just 7 km south of Mt Cook Village, T03-430 8034, T0800-800702, skiplanes.co.nz. This flight-seeing option offers snow-landings high up on the Tasman Glacier, from $340.

Twizel *p38*
Heli-bikes
Heli-bike Twizel, T03-435 0626, T0800-435424, helibike.com. Wild rides range from 1½-3½ hrs and cost $55-200.

❷ Transport

Kaikoura *p32, map p34*
For travel information and bookings contact the i-SITE visitor centre.

Train
Trains serve **Blenheim** and the West Coast (Greymouth), T0800-872467, tranzscenic.co.nz

The West Coast

The west coast of the South Island is a land of extremes: extreme climate, extreme geography, extreme ecosystems and, above all, extreme scenery. It is a place of majestic beauty. Bounded on one side by the Tasman Sea and on the other by the heady peaks of the Southern Alps, it encompasses a narrow stretch of land that accounts for only 8% of the total landmass of New Zealand. Between these boundaries lies a quarter of all New Zealand's native forest, a lush and predominantly impenetrable landscape copiously watered by an average annual rainfall of more than 5 m. The boundaries of five of the country's 14 national parks breach the west coast region. Two of these, Paparoa National Park and the Westland National Park, it can call its very own, with the latter boasting the huge Fox and Franz Josef glaciers.

The settlements in the region, strung along the 600-km length of SH6, from Karamea in the north to Jackson's Bay in the south, are not attractive places and stand in stark contrast to the beauty surrounding them. Nature, thankfully, has never made it easy for people to live here nor plunder its resources. The modern-day West Coast is sparsely populated, housing less than 1% of the country's total population. Indeed, there are fewer people living here now than in the late 19th century.

Most visitors tackle the West Coast from North to south and either via the Buller Gorge from Nelson, Lewis Pass from Hanmer or Arthur's Pass from Christchurch. As usual what you see and what you do here will depend on time, but unfortunately you must now add another more crucial factor – the weather. Beware, for many, the West Coast can alter the perception of what proper rain really is and what 'rain stopped play' really means.

Westport

ⓘ *For regional details contact the Westport i-SITE visitor centre, 1 Brougham St, T03-7896658, westport.org.nz, daily 0900-1800, winter 0900-1600.*

Westport, the west coast's oldest town, is not a pretty place. On first acquaintance, its flat expanse of unimaginative, orderly and treeless blocks are uninspiring to say the least. But if the place lacks soul, its people do not. They retain the proud and stoic traditions of the old pioneers and coal miners: the down-to-earth working-class attitude, the warm welcome and the humour. Westport is often used as an overnight base before heading north to Karamea and the Heaphy Track or south towards Greymouth. There, however, are a few attractions and activities that may detain you, including rafting on the **Buller River** and a large fur seal colony at **Cape Foulwind** (11 km).

The **Coaltown Museum** ⓘ *Queen St South, T03-7898204, daily 0900-1630, $10, child $5,* has an interesting range of displays covering the history of coal mining in the region, while the **West Coast Brewery** ⓘ *10 Lyndhurst St, T03-789 6253, free tastings Mon-Sat,* offers tastings of various heady brews including the popular 'Good Bastards'.

Karamea

From Westport, SH67 heads north to Karamea (100 km), a former 'frontier' settlement of Karamea, perched on its namesake river mouth and overshadowed by the rising peaks of the **Kahurangi National Park**. It is a pleasant and peaceful place and most often used as a base for the famed **Heaphy Track**, which begins at the road terminus 15 km north. Walking part of its first section offers a great day walk. Karamea also has some lesser-known sights nearby that are quite simply superb, in particular the limestone caves and arches of the **Oparara Basin**. Bones have been discovered in the caves belonging to the now extinct moa and the New Zealand eagle that had a 3-m wingspan. If you have time (or even if you do not, make the time) go and see them.

For detail and directions contact the **Karamea i-SITE Visitor Centre and Resource Centre** ⓘ *Bridge St, just as you come into the village, T03-7826652, karameainfo.co.nz, daily 0900-1700.* It also has internet, can organize activities and issues DoC hut passes.

Punakaiki and the Paparoa National Park

From Westport SH6 begins its relentless 600-km journey south, down the length of the west coast. The pretty coastal enclave of Punakaiki sits on the coast and the boundary of the Paparoa National Park 60 km south of Westport and 50 km north of Greymouth. Designated in 1987, Paparoa covers a relatively small area (by New Zealand standards) of 30,000 ha and features a predominantly karst (limestone) topography. From mountain to coast, the park has everything from limestone bluffs to dramatic overhangs and caves. The most visited feature in the park are the pancake rocks and blowholes of **Dolomite Point** accessed from Punakaiki (20 minutes). There are some notable walks including the **Truman Track**, which begins beside SH6, 3 km north of Punakaiki. It is a beautiful 15-minute stroll through coastal rainforest and nikau palms that delivers you peacefully on the sands and rocky outcrops of Perpendicular Point.

Kayaking and horse trekking are two other popular activities in the area.

For detail contact the **DoC Paparoa National Park visitor centre** ⓘ *SH6, Punakaiki, T03-731 1895, doc.govt.nz, punakaiki.co.nz, daily 0900-1800, winter 0900-1630.*

Renderusinsanitus

There is no collective noun that adequately describes Renderusinsanitus (as they call it on the West Coast) - that heinous, insect equivalent to Hannibal Lecter – the New Zealand sandfly. Venture anywhere west of the main divide of the South Island and you will, without fail, not only encounter vast squadrons of them but also unconsciously enter into a state of perpetual war against them.

There are not one, but 13 species of sandfly (or blackfly) in New Zealand. Fortunately though, only two of the species actually bite, but unfortunately, you are still hopelessly outnumbered. You may (or indeed may not) be surprised to learn that it is only the female that bites. Apparently they need a good feed of blood in order to lay their eggs.

Biting is at its peak just after dawn or before dusk on warm, overcast, low pressure days, especially when humidity is high. Your only saviour is wind. It is due to the high rainfall that sandflies are so prevalent on the West Coast and in Fiordland.

You will find a number of expensive insect repellents readily available throughout the region. Those that contain DEET are the most effective.

Greymouth and around

From Punakaiki the coast road continues its relentless route south, treating you to some fine coastal scenery, before turning inland through Runanga to meet the Grey River and the west coast's largest commercial centre – Greymouth. The Grey River Valley receives some of the heaviest rainfall in the country and on more than one occasion the town has been badly flooded. On initial acquaintance Greymouth seems to share the drab aesthetics of most northern west coast towns and certainly lives up to its uninspiring name. That said, the people of Greymouth are welcoming, friendly and certainly not short of heart or colour. Today, the town is mostly used by tourists as a short stopover point or supply base for further investigations of the coast. It is also the terminus of the **TranzAlpine** ① T0800-872467, tranzscenic.co.nz, scenic train journey through Arthurs Pass from Christchurch – a major attraction in itself. There are a few local attractions and some exciting activities on offer from whitewater and cave rafting to quad biking and brewery tours. Inland from Greymouth, the small satellite towns of **Blackball** and **Reefton** are the main highlights along the watershed of the Grey River Valley and provide further evidence of the regions gold and coal mining past. It was in Blackball in the early 1900s that the Labour and Trade Union movements were first formed in New Zealand. Further south the peaceful surroundings of **Lake Brunner** are a stark contrast to the highly commercial 'Shantytown' a working replica of an 1880s gold mining settlement.

For information contact the **Greymouth i-SITE visitor centre** ① corner of Mackay and Herbert streets, T03-7685101, greydistrict.co.nz, Mon-Fri 0830-1900, Sat 0900-1800, Sun 1000-1700. **Travel Centre** ① railway station, 164 Mackay St, T03-768 7080.

Hokitika

More gold passed through Hokitika (or 'Hoki') in the 1860s than any other town on the coast. Between 1865 and 1867, over 37,000 hopefuls arrived requiring a staggering 84 hotels to put them all up in. In those heady days it seemed only the river itself could hold the town back. At one point during the gold rush there was at least one grounding every 10 weeks – and 21 in 1865 alone. Like everywhere else of course the gold soon ran out and old 'Hoki' slipped into rapid decline. But today gold has been replaced by that other precious resource – tourism. It is now the craft capital of the west coast and summer sees crowds of visitors arrive by the busload, to watch glass-blowing and greenstone carving and to browse in its numerous galleries concentrated along Tancred Street.

Inland from Hokitika (14 km) is the picturesque **Lake Kaniere**, a popular haven in summer for swimming, watersports, picnicking and walking. Also accessed directly from Hokitika (33 km) via the settlements of Kaniere and Kokatahi (end of Kowhitirangi and Whitcombe Road) or, alternatively, via Lake Kaniere (loop road to Kokatahi) is the picturesque and moody **Hokitika Gorge**. Other than the impressive scenery the highlight here is the swing-bridge that after heavy rains, makes the crossing an exciting prospect.

For regional information contact the **Westland i-SITE visitor centre** ① *Carnegie Building, corner of Hamilton and Tancred streets, T03-755 6166, hokitika.org.nz, west-coast. co.nz.nz, daily in summer 0830-1800, winter Mon-Fri 0830-1700, Sat-Sun 1000-1600.*

South to Franz Josef
South from Hokitika the influence of humanity decreases dramatically and the aesthetics begin to reflect the sheer dominance of nature. Mountain ranges climb steadily on the eastern horizon towards the heady peaks of the Westland National Park and to Mount Cook itself. Small villages like Ross and Harihari cling precariously to a history of gold mining and demonstrate in size alone how much nature rules these parts, and hopefully always will. For many this is where the real west coast begins.

Pukekura and the Puke Pub
① *T03-7554144, pukekura.co.nz.*
About 18 km south of Ross is the small settlement of Pukekura, population 2. It began as a hotel on the stage coach trail south, had a saw mill for a while in the 1950s before Peter Salter and his partner Justine Giddy establishment the **Bushman's Centre** in 1993. The place is instantly recognizable and notorious for the giant **sandfly** that hangs with menace from its walls. As well as a fine café (with its superb 'road kill soup of the day') and shop it has a great little interactive museum ($4), where you can learn about bush craft, meet live possums (one that have not been turned in to pies that is), stroke a pig, then wantonly throw sharp knives and axes at the wall. It's brilliant. Other activities based at the centre include horse trekking and gold panning.

Across the road from the centre is the famed (and unfortunately named) Puke Pub where you can do your bit for conservation and indulge in a possum pie.

Whataroa
Whataroa, 35 km southwest of Harihari, provides an opportunity to see the revered white heron or **kotuku** congregated at their sole New Zealand breeding rookery. The birds are only in residence from mid-October to mid-March. **White Heron Sanctuary Tours** ① *T03-753 4120, T0800-523456, white herontours.co.nz, tours $122, child $55, page 46,* offers a 2½-hour tour by jet boat to access the hide that overlooks the colony.

While in Whataroa don't miss the **Kotuku Gallery** ① *Main St, T03-753 4249,* regarded as one of the best Maori galleries in the country.

Okarito
Okarito, a small coastal settlement and former goldfields port, is 13 km off SH6 and 15 km south of Whataroa. This beautiful little paradise, set beachside next to the vast 3240-ha

Okarito Lagoon backed by stunning views of the Southern Alps, is not surprisingly the favourite haunt of many a New Zealander. Thankfully most people shoot past the road junction from SH6 in their rush to see their first glacier – Franz Josef – 29 km to the south. But for those who take the time and the diversion, they will be rewarded not only with Okarito's simple do-nothing appeal, but also some excellent walking, kayaking and birdwatching opportunities. There is no public transport to Okarito and no shops in Okarito so take your own supplies. Across the road from the obviously historic and incredibly cute youth hostel is the almost unsightly **obelisk** commemorating Abel Tasman's first sighting of New Zealand, somewhere off Okarito in 1642. For a walk try the steady climb (1½ hours) via the old, but well-formed, pack track through native bush to the **Okarito Trig**. On a clear day it affords a stunning view across the bush-clad hills to the Southern Alps.

The West Coast listings

For hotel and restaurant price codes and other relevant information, see pages 9-13.

⊜ Where to stay

Karamea *p42*
$$$ Rough and Tumble Bush Lodge, Mokihinui River, 5 mins from Seddonville Pub (50 km north of Westport), T03-732 1337, roughandtumble.co.nz. Classic and affordable bush lodge accommodation overlooking the Mokihinui River. 5 cosy en suites with memorable views. Furnishings of native timber abound and an outdoor campfire, swimming hole and bush bath all add to the appeal. Excellent in-house cuisine. It is remote but well worth the effort.

Punakaiki and the Paparoa National Park *p42*
$$ Hydrangea Cottages, north of the centre, Punakaiki T03-731 1839, pancake-rocks.co.nz. Quality self-contained cottages. Very cute and reasonably priced.

Motor parks
$$-$ Punakaiki Beach Camp, Owen St (off SH6), Punakaiki, T03-731 1894, holidayparks. co.nz/punakaiki. Set next to the beach and only a short walk from the main village. It offers spacious grounds, cabins and powered/tent sites, camp kitchen.

Greymouth and around *p43*
Motor parks
$$$-$ Top Ten Greymouth Holiday Park, 2 Chesterfield St, T03-768 6618, T0800-867104, top10greymouth.co.nz. Spacious, alongside the beach, with full facilities.

Hokitika *p43*
$$$ Beachfront Hotel, 111 Revell St, T03-755 8344, beachfronthotel.com. Modern, well facilitated with standard to luxury, most en suite and some with ocean views. A reputable restaurant/bar overlooking the beach.

Motor parks
$$-$ Shining Star Log Chalets and Motor Camp, 16 Richards Dr, T03-755 8921, shining@xtra.co.nz. A fine motel/ motor park with tidy self-contained lodges designed and built by the owners. It is close to the beach in a quiet location and also takes campervans and tents. Full facilities.

Okarito *p44*
Motor parks
$$-$ Okarito YHA Hostel and DoC campsite, Palmerston St, T0800-278299, yha.co.nz. Something of novelty set in the former 1870s schoolhouse. Bookings can be made via the Franz Josef i-SITE or payment made at the warden's house close to the hostel. Coin-operated showers at the basic DoC campground opposite where fires are

permitted. Beware of sandflies and take insect repellent.

🍴 Restaurants

Westport p42
$$ Bay House Café, southern end of Tauranga Bay, Cape Foulwind (near Westport), T03-789 7133, thebayhouse.co.nz. The best local restaurant, offering breakfast, lunch and an à la carte menu for dinner and in a superb setting overlooking the bay and within walking distance of the seal colony.

Greymouth p43
$$ Jade Boulder Café, 1 Guinness St, T03-768 0700. Good daytime option attached to the Jade Country shop – an attraction in itself. Serves the West Coast delicacy whitebait year round.

Hokitika p43
$$$-$$ Café de Paris, 19 Tancred St, T03-755 8933. Daily from 0830. Award-winning restaurant with imaginative French/Italian influenced à la carte dinner and changing blackboard menu for breakfast and lunch.

❄ Festivals

Hokitika p43
Mar Hokitika Wildfoods Festival, T03-755 8321, wildfoods.co.nz. Hokitika enjoys such a human influx that it can jog the memories of the gold rush days at this mighty party dressed up as a 'wild' food event. On offer is a vast array of culinary delights from possum pies to witchetty bugs. There's even the odd testicle – yum!

⚲ What to do

Westport p42
Tour operators
Underworld Adventures, Charlestown, 27 km south of Westport, T0800-116686, caverafting.com. Offers tours, caving and rafting trips to the Te Tahi and Metro limestone caves in Paparoa National Park.

Whataroa p44
White Heron Sanctuary Tours, T03-753 4120, T0800-523456, white herontours. co.nz. Offers a 2½-hr tour by jet boat to access the hide that overlooks the colony, tours $122, child $55.

Okarito p44
Kayaking
Okarito Nature Tours, T03-753 4014, okarito.co.nz. Kayak rental and guided trips to explore the scenery and natural history of the lagoon and its many channels, from $80.

⊖ Transport

Westport p42
Car
Heading north or south be sure to fill up your tank in Greymouth or Westport as there is no petrol station in Punakaiki.

The Glacier Region

To add to New Zealand's majestic scenery and ecological surprises, the two gigantic and dynamic monoliths of ice – Franz Josef and Fox Glaciers – provide a dramatic sight. They are the brightest jewels in the highly decorated crown of the Westland and Mount Cook national parks, joined, yet separated on the map, by the jagged summits and peaks of the Southern Alps and the Great Dividing Range. In summer there are two moods to the neighbouring villages of Franz and Fox. When the sun shines they are a frenetic buzz of activity: from the moment the sun peeks over the mountains, the skies fill with the sound of aircraft, the roads swarm with tour buses and the streets fill with expectant tourists, consumed with the desire to get to the glaciers, walk on them and photograph them. And yet, when the clouds gather (which is often) and the rain descends (or rather crashes down), the pace of everything slows, dramatically: the air hangs heavy with silence, the streets fill with puddles and the tourists' glum faces stare out from behind café windows. The average annual rainfall in the area is 5 m, over 180 rain days, and at Franz and Fox it's amazing just how much the weather and two multi-million, ton blocks of ice can dictate. However, it's not all bad, there are many clear, sunny days too – an average of 1860 sunshine hours annually, more than in many other regions in New Zealand. Plan to give yourself at least two days in the area and always book your accommodation well in advance. If you have scenic flights booked, these can be forwarded if it's cloudy.

Franz Josef

Franz Josef owes its very existence and, of course its name, to the great block of ice that sits 5 km south of the village. Of the two principally tourist-based settlements (Franz and Fox), Franz is the larger and better serviced. As you might expect it is very much a seasonal destination, crowded in summer, quiet in winter.

Franz Josef – the glacier – was first sighted and officially documented by both Abel Tasman in 1642 and Cook in 1770, but first properly explored and named by geologist and explorer Julius von Haast in 1865. When he first explored its lower reaches it was almost 3 km nearer the coast than it is today. The official title of 'Francis Joseph Glacier' was given in honour of the Emperor Franz Josef of Austria. The spelling was later changed to Franz Josef in accordance with the internationally accepted version.

From the car park (along Glacier Access Road) it is a 1½-hour return walk alongside the wide and rocky **Waiho River** bed to within 500 m of the glacier face. Unless properly equipped you cannot walk on the glacier itself; to do that you are strongly advised to join a guided **glacier walking trip**. The 280-m-high viewpoint on **Sentinel Rock** (a remnant of previous glacial erosion) is perhaps the best place to view the glacier from afar; it is easily accessed from near the main car park (20 minutes). But perhaps the best way to view the glacier and the peaks that crown it is from the air and there are numerous **scenic flight** options available. If the weather is fine do not miss the opportunity to do so. At the very least take a heli-flight that involves a snow landing. To experience the silence up there is as memorable as the scenery.

Franz Josef i-SITE visitor centre ⓘ *Main Rd, Franz Josef, T03-752 0796, doc.govt.nz*, has displays, information on walks and up-to-date weather forecasts. On Main Road numerous outlets also provides local information, arrange transport and offer activity bookings and internet.

Fox Glacier

Many people visiting the Glacier Region only visit one of the great monoliths, with Franz Josef being the most favoured. However, if you have time, Fox Glacier (25 km south of Franz and a further 8 km southeast) is no less dramatic. The Fox Glacier Valley and the chilly Fox River which surges from the glacier terminus, provide a significantly different atmosphere. The Fox Glacier was originally called the Victoria Glacier and was renamed in honour of former New Zealand Prime Minister, Sir William Fox, on a visit in 1872. The small village of Fox Glacier is the main service centre and sits on a site that was, as recently as 5000 years ago, covered by the present glacier.

Although less commercial, Fox, like its neighbour Franz, can be explored independently at its terminus, but you will need a guide to walk or climbed on it. Once again, however, the recommendation is to admire it from the air. There are a number of interesting walks within the valley, at the coast and around the reflective **Lake Matheson**, which lies 4 km west of the village – but at dawn and dusk don't expect solitude. Again the **DoC office** ⓘ *Main Rd, T03-7510807*, is the best source of unbiased information.

South to Haast

From Fox Glacier you leave the great glaciers and towering peaks of the national parks behind and SH6 winds its scenic way ever southwards to Haast and to the most remote region of the west coast: South Westland. For many years Fox was as far south as any tourist ventured, the road from there becoming rough and eventually non-existent at Paringa. With the opening of the great Haast Pass Highway in 1965 the two roads were linked making the continuous journey possible. Given the terrain in South Westland, it is not hard to understand why such a link was so late in coming. Despite the intrusion, much of South Westland remains remote, unspoilt and remarkably beautiful.

The reflective waters of **Lake Moeraki** are a further 18 km south of Lake Paringa and from there SH6 rejoins the coast and climbs to **Knight Point** with its spectacular views of sea stacks and near inaccessible beaches. It was just south of Knight Point that the Haast Highway was officially opened in 1965, thereby connecting Otago with south Westland and the west coast proper. A little further south is easy access to the beach at **Ship Creek**. Here you can choose from a number of excellent short walks to explore the beach, coastal forest and a small lake held captive by the dunes. From Ship Creek SH6 hugs the coast and passes some spectacular examples of coastal rimu, rata and kahikatea forest on its approach to Haast and the 750-m **Haast River Bridge**.

Haast

The Haast Region of South Westland contains some of the most unspoiled ecosystems in New Zealand. The stunning scenery, from mountaintop to coastal plain, includes pristine streams that flow into vast river mouths fringed with dense tracts of ancient coastal (Kahikatea) forests. Within the forest lie swamps and hidden lakes and all along their fringe are endless swathes of beach covered in sculpted driftwood. On the coastal plain the annual rainfall, at 5 m, is similar to that of much of the west coast. But above 1500 m, the average can be over three times that and, after a deluge, the great river can turn into a menacing torrent to which so many ravaged tree trunks attest.

Haast Junction (before Haast itself) is home to the DoC visitor centre, a petrol station and the World Heritage Hotel. A further 4 km south of Haast Junction, on the Jackson's Bay Road, is Haast Beach, another small conglomerate, including another petrol station, a motel, food store and some private homes. From there the road continues for 50 km before reaching a dead end and the remote village of **Jackson's Bay**. East of there an unsealed road accesses the **Arawata River** and the **Cascade Saddle**, in itself a memorable day trip.

Other than scenic drives and walks other activities in the area include the popular **jet boating** trips up the Haast and Walatoto Rivers. And what a delightful name **Waiatoto** is. Now you know what to scream out in Maori the next time you stub your toe. It actually means 'red waters'.

For local information contact the **DoC Haast visitor centre** ⓘ *Jnc. SH6 and Jackson Bay Road, Haast, T03-750 0809, doc.govt.nz.*

Haast Pass

From Haast Township SH6 turns inland and follows the bank of the Haast River before being enveloped by mountains and surmounting what was, until 1960, insurmountable. The Haast Pass at 563 m is an ancient Maori greenstone trail known as Tiori-patea, which means 'the way ahead is clear'. Ironically, being the principal water catchment of the Haast River and plagued by frequent floods and landslips, the name is one of misplaced optimism as the modern-day road can testify. However, although sometimes treacherous and difficult to negotiate, the crossing captures the mood of the place, with names such as the **Valley of Darkness** and **Mount Awful**. Even beside the road there is suggestion of this, with other evocative titles like Solitary Creek No 2 and the first of three waterfalls, **Roaring Billy** 28 km inland from Haast. A further 25 km another waterfall – the competitively named **Thunder Creek Falls** – drop a vertical 28 m into the Haast River. They can be accessed from a short loop track beside the road.

The gorge, known as the **Gates of Haast,** is just a little further on and you can see the huge boulders and precipitous rock walls that proved such a barrier to road construction for so many years. Above the Gates the road and the river level off before the Haast Pass itself and the boundary of Westland and Otago. From here the scenery dramatically changes and you leave the mighty West Coast behind.

The Glacier Region listings

For hotel and restaurant price codes and other relevant information, see pages 9-13.

⊖ Where to stay

Franz Josef *p48*
$$$$ Franz Josef Glacier Country Retreat, off SH6, 6 km north of Franz Josef, T03-752 0012, glacier-retreat.co.nz. A replica of a traditional west-coast homestead in a peaceful farmland setting, owned by a 4th generation west coast family. 12 luxury en suite rooms with a historical edge. 4-poster beds and claw-foot or spa baths adds to the appeal.

Motor parks
$$-$ Rainforest Retreat Holiday Park, Cron St, T0800-873346, T03-7520220, rainforestretreat.co.nz. Affordable eco-based log cabins in a quiet setting, yet still close to the village. The various options include studios and family units. There are also campervan facilities and tent sites, with modern facilities including a camp kitchen. Spa and internet.

Fox Glacier *p48*
$$$$ Te Weheka Inn, opposite the DoC/VIC, Main Rd, T03-7510730, teweheka.co.nz. Pitched somewhere between a motel and a luxury boutique hotel. It has a striking design and offers modern suites. Tariff includes breakfast.

Motor parks
$$-$ Fox Glacier Holiday Park, Cooks Flat Rd, T03-751 0821. The main motor park in the village. Spacious, it has all the usual

facilities including cabins, lodge rooms, flats, powered/tent sites and a backpacker dorm. Good facilities.

Haast *p49*
$$$ Heartland World Heritage Hotel, corner of SH6 and Jackson's Bay Rd, Haast Junction, T0800-502444, T03-750 0828, world-heritage-hotel.com. Long-established and recently refurbished, it has 54 en suite units from standard to family, but is best known for its restaurant and bar. The open log fire is particularly attractive.

Motor parks
$$-$ Haast Beach Holiday Park, Okuru (15 km south), Jackson's Bay Rd, T03-750 0860, accommodationhaastpark.co.nz. Offers a number of basic motel units, self-contained and standard cabins, but is mainly noted for its location, friendliness and fine modern kitchen and lounge facilities.

⊘ Restaurants

Franz Josef *p48*
$$ The Blue Ice Café & Pub, Main Rd, T03-752 0707. Serves good pizza upstairs and à la carte dining on the ground level. All-out war on the free pool table is its other speciality.

Fox Glacier *p48*
$$ The Plateau Cafe & Bar, corner Sullivan Rd and Main Rd, T03-751 0058. Daily from 1100. Modern decor with open fire and a wide-ranging à la carte menu including hot curries – perfect after a day clambering over a glacier or walking in the rain.

Haast *p49*
$ Cray Pot Café, T03-750 0035, Jackson's Bay. Daily 1030-1900. Well, it's the end of the road folks – a long way but worth it. A quirky cross between a rail carriage and a barge serving fish and chips. You can eat in (recommended) or take away, but beware of the sandflies.

● What to do

Scenic flights
Flights start at around $95 for a 10-min flight. A snow landing is recommended. There are several companies including: **Helicopter Line**, Main Rd, T0800-807767, helicopter.co.nz. Flights from 20-40 mins and a 3-hr heli-hike option.
Mountain Helicopters, T03-751 0045, T0800-369423, mountainhelicopters.co.nz. Flights from both Franz and Fox from 10-40 mins. Good company with cheaper rates.
Mount Cook Ski Plane Adventures (Aoraki Mt Cook), Main Rd, T03-752 074, mtcookskiplanes.com. Offering the only fixed-wing glacier landings in New Zealand.

Sky diving
Skydive Glacier Country, T0800-751 0080, skydivingnz.co.nz. Offers tandems amidst some of the country's most stunning scenery.

Franz Josef *p48*
Glacier trips
Franz Josef Glacier Guides, Main Rd, T03-752 0763, T0800-484337, franzjosef glacier.com. A highly experienced outfit offering 4- to 8-hr glacier excursions as well as heli-hike and high-level alpine trips, from $66.50.

Fox Glacier *p48*
Glacier walking
Fox Glacier Guiding, Alpine Guides Building, Main Rd, T03-751 0825, T0800-111600, foxguides.co.nz. Offers 2- to 8-hr excursions as well as heli-hike, ice climbing, mountaineering and alpine-hut trips, from $49.

Haast *p49*
River safaris
Haast River Safaris, the 'Red Barn' between Haast Junction and Haast Township, T0800-865382, haastriver.co.nz. River safari up the Haast River Valley. The 1½-hr trips on its purpose-built jet boat depart daily at 0900, 1100 and 1400 and cost from $139, child $59.

Contents

Footprint features

Marlborough & Nelson

Marlborough

As the ferry slides into port at Picton, Queen Charlotte Sound seems like a giant foyer. The vast convoluted system of drowned river valleys, peninsulas and islets that make up the Sound's 1500 km of coastline are often dubbed New Zealand's 'little slice of Norway' and throughout its watery maze you can enjoy stunning scenery, cruising, tramping, kayaking, wildlife watching or just a few days' peaceful relaxation. The two main tourist bases for the Sounds are Picton, at the terminus of Queen Charlotte Sound, and also Havelock, at the terminus of Pelorus Sound.

There are only two access points and tricky road networks. The first is at Linkwater on the Queen Charlotte Drive between Picton and Havelock – itself a very pretty, but winding drive. From there you can access the bays of Kenepuru and Queen Charlotte Sounds as well as Endeavour Inlet, where Captain Cook came ashore. The second is at Rai Valley with access to points on the Tennyson Inlet and to French Pass. If you do not have much time, settle for a water-based trip from Picton or Havelock and perhaps a night's stay at one of the many excellent and remote accommodations. Or, if you are Nelson-bound, take a day to explore the road to French Pass with its stunning views and tidal maelstrom.

Marlborough Sounds

Although most of what the Sounds has to offer is easily accessed by boat, it is also possible to explore much of it on foot. There are two popular tramping tracks, the 71-km, three- to five-day, **Queen Charlotte Track** and the lesser-known 27 km, two-day **Nydia Track**.

The Queen Charlotte can be tackled in several ways, by foot (of course), but also in combination with mountain bike and/or kayak. There are DoC huts and plenty of independent accommodation establishments to suit all budgets along the way and you can even have your pack delivered en route by water taxi. Again all the fine detail is available from the i-SITE. The Nydia is more rugged and far less facilitated, which may of course suit the more traditional tramper.

Picton

The pretty township of Picton, gateway to the Marlborough Sounds and the South Island, is in summer a buzz of activity with eager visitors coming and going by ferry, car and train, or heading out in to the Sounds in all manner of crafts. But in winter it reverts to its more familiar role as a sleepy port, the ferry terminal café frequented by rotund lorry drivers on the ol'familiar inter-island run dripping ketchup as they demolish a mushy meat pie. There

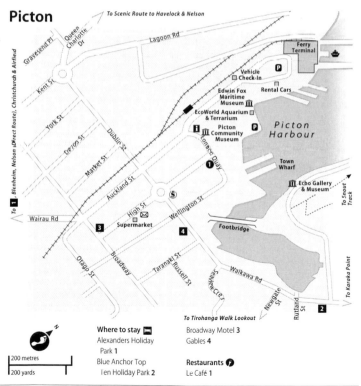

Picton

Where to stay 🛏
Alexanders Holiday Park **1**
Blue Anchor Top Ten Holiday Park **2**
Broadway Motel **3**
Gables **4**

Restaurants 🍴
Le Café **1**

are a few sights in Picton, nothing spectacular. Remember you are on the South Island now, where sights become the domain of the nature-made, not the man-made. For most new arrivals, quite rightly, the first major sight is the activities board in the visitor centre. Cruising, dolphin watching, island trips, kayaking, mountain biking, tramping or just plain 'where's the best hammock with a view' – it's all on offer and the range is a little daunting.

Perhaps while you are thinking about it you should take a muse at the **Edwin Fox Maritime Museum** ① *Dunbar Wharf, T03-5736868, edwinfoxsociety.com, daily 0900-1700, $6*, between the ferry terminal and the town centre. There the remains of the 1853, once fully rigged East India Trading ship is being lovingly restored to a reminder of her former glory by the Edwin Fox Society. The vessel, which is (apparently) the ninth oldest ship in the world and the only remaining example of her type, was a troop carrier in the Crimean War before being commissioned to bring immigrants to Australia and New Zealand. Also here is Roofliss, an amphibious converted van which has successfully crossed the Cook Strait.

In front of the museum is the **EcoWorld Aquarium & Terrarium** ① *T03-573 6030, ecoworldnz.co.nz, daily 1000-1730, day pass $22, child $10*. As one of the few aquariums in the country it is perhaps worth a look, but more fun for kids. A range of displays house the usual characters including an octopus called Larry, some seahorses, rays, the local 'living fossil' – the tuatara (reptile) and last but by no means least a big tank of squid soup.

i-SITE visitor centre ① *The Foreshore, T03-520 3113, destinationmarlborough.com, daily 0830-1800 (1700 winter)*.

Blenheim and the Marlborough vineyards

Although it is depressingly flat and unremarkable looking, Blenheim, Marlborough's largest town, is a popular tourist base, primarily for those intent on sampling the region's fine wines. Most of the wineries lie just to the west of town and around the satellite village of Renwick 12 km west, on the fertile soils of the **Wairau Plains**. Marlborough is New Zealand's largest wine-growing region and forms the start (or finish) of the **Classic New Zealand Wine Trail** that tipples its way through Wellington and the Wairarapa to the Hawes Bay, classicwinetrail.co.nz.

There are over 50 wineries around Blenheim and Renwick producing highly acclaimed Chardonnay, Riesling, Cabernet Sauvignon, Merlot, Pinot Noir, sparkling Methode Champenoise and some best Sauvignon Blanc in the world. Montana sowed the first seeds of success in the early 1970s and is now the largest winery in the country. Three decades on, Montana has been joined by other world-famous names like Cloudy Bay and Villa Maria and has become a major national export industry.

Like Hawke's Bay in the North Island, the wineries have been quick to take advantage of the tourist dollar, with most offering tours, tastings (free or small charge) and good restaurants. Although the competition in Marlborough is fierce, the region's vineyards lack the architectural splendour or variety of Hawke's Bay. Perhaps they just leave the wine to do the talking.

If you are a complete novice it's a good idea to join one of the many excellent tours on offer. They generally last a full or half-day, taking in the pick of the crop and the widest variety of wine types. There is always an informative commentary, often a lunch stop and, of course, numerous tastings included in the package. If you know a bit about wines and have particular tastes, many tour operators will create a personal itinerary. If you wish to explore by yourself, there are plenty of maps and leaflets at the **i-SITE visitor centre** ① *Railway Station, SH1, T03-577 8080, destinationmarlborough.com, winemarlborough.net. nz, daily 0830-1830; winter Mon-Fri 0830-1800, Sat-Sun 0900-1600*.

Blenheim

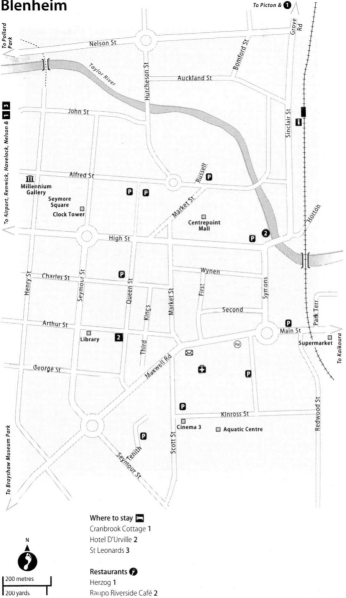

To Picton & **1**

Grove Rd

Nelson St

To Pollard Park

Taylor River

Hutcheson St

Bomford St

Auckland St

Sinclair St

i

John St

To Airport, Renwick, Havelock, Nelson & **1** **3**

Alfred St

Russell

P

Millennium Gallery

Seymore Square

Clock Tower

P **P**

Market St

Centrepoint Mall

P **2**

Horton

High St

Henry St

Charles St

Seymour St

P

Queen St

Wynen

First

Symons

Arthur St

Kings

Market St

Second

Main St

P

Park Terr

To Kaikoura

Supermarket

Library

2

Third

Maxwell Rd

✉

Pol

George St

✚

P

Kinross St

Redwood St

P

Cinema 3

Aquatic Centre

To Brayshaw Museum Park

Tenith

Seymour St

Scott St

N

200 metres

200 yards

Where to stay 🛏
Cranbrook Cottage **1**
Hotel D'Urville **2**
St Leonards **3**

Restaurants 🍴
Herzog **1**
Raupo Riverside Café **2**

Wineries around Blenheim

A comprehensive list of the wineries is beyond the scope of this guide, but some wineries of particular note are listed below. The best time to visit the vineyards is in April when the heavily laden vines are ripe for the picking. See also **Winery tours**, page 61.

Allan Scott Estate, Jackson's Rd, T03-572 9054, allanscott.com. Daily 0900-1700. Established in 1973, producing fine Sauvignon, Chardonnay and Riesling wines. The Twelve Trees restaurant, is a deservedly popular lunch venue, open daily from 0900.

Cloudy Bay, Jackson's Rd, T03-520 9147, cloudybay.co.nz. Tastings and tours daily 1000-1700. An internationally famous label with a loyal following particularly for its Sauvignon Blanc.

Herzog, 81 Jeffries Rd, T03-572 8770, herzog.co.nz. Daily 1100-1500. Not only fine wine (particularly Pinot Noir) but also one of the best winery restaurants, Oct-mid May. Exceptional international wine list.

Highfield Estate, Brookby Rd, T03-572 9244, highfield.co.nz. Daily 1000-1700. Fine wine, architecture and the best view of the lot from its rampart tower. Reputable indoor/outdoor restaurant open daily for lunch 1130-1530.

Hunters Wines, Rapaura Rd, T03-572 8489, hunters.co.nz. Another of the larger, most popular labels and home to one of the world's most renowned female vintners, Jane Hunter. Also noted for its gardens and café (open weekdays 1030-1630).

Johanneshof Cellars, SH1, Koromiko, 20 km north of Blenheim, T03-573 7035, johanneshof.co.nz. Summer Tue-Sun 1000-1600. Cellar tours. Boutique vineyard famous for its underground 'rock cellars', lined with both barrel and bottle.

Montana Brancott Winery, Main South Rd (SH1), just to the south of Blenheim, T03-578 2099, montanawines.com. Daily 0900-1700. It is almost rude not to visit this, the largest wine producer in the country. The new visitor centre is very impressive and there are half-hourly tours (1000-1500), tastings, a restaurant with outdoor seating and a classy shop. This is also the venue for the now world-famous **Marlborough Food and Wine Festival** in Feb (see page 60).

Prenzel Distillery, Sheffield St, Riverlands Estate, T03-520 8215, prenzel.com. Something different – New Zealand's 1st commercial fruit distillery producing a range of fruit liqueurs, schnapps, and brandies.

Seresin, 85 Bedford Rd, Renwick, T03-572 9408, seresin.co.nz. Summer daily 1000-1630, winter Mon-Fri 1000-1630. Noted not only for its wine, but also its artwork. That has to be one of the best logos of any label.

Te Whare Ra, 56 Anglesea St, Renwick, T03-572 8581, te-whare-ra.co.nz. Small family-run boutique operation with a fine reputation and a wide range.

Marlborough listings

For hotel and restaurant price codes and other relevant information, see pages 9-13.

● Where to stay

Marlborough Sounds *p55*
$$$$ Bay of Many Coves Resort, Queen Charlotte Sound, T03-579 9771, bayofmanycovesresort.co.nz. Represents the Sounds at its best. Remote seclusion yet all the comforts of a modern award-winning resort. Classy studio units and apartments with memorable views across the sound, café, restaurant and a wide range of activities from kayaking to heli-fishing.

$$$-$ Hopewell, Kenepuru Sound, T03-573 4341, hopewell.co.nz. Excellent establishment in a remote location on Kenepuru Sound, providing the perfect blend of value and comfort. Although accessible by road from Havelock North or Picton it is a tortuous drive. A water taxi is recommended and adds the overall experience, or you can fly direct from Wellington (Soundsair) to the local airfield from where you can be picked up. A range of options from a self-contained cottage to doubles and four-shares. Attractive grounds right down to the water's edge. Outdoor spa overlooking the sound, internet, kayaks and plenty of water-based activities, with fishing trips a speciality.

$$-$ Lochmara Lodge (Backpackers), Lochmara Bay, Queen Charlotte Bay, T03-573 4554, lochmara lodge.co.nz. A deservingly popular eco-oriented backpacker hostel with a great, laid-back atmosphere. Dorm and private studio chalets (some en suite). If you can remove yourself from a hammock there is a spa, licensed restaurant/café, open fire, free kayak and windsurf hire. Excellent in-house eco-trips to Motuara Island.

Picton *p55, map p55*
$$$ The Broadway Motel, 113 High St, T03-573 6563, broadwaymotel.co.nz. Centrally located and handy for the ferry terminal the Broadway is one of the most modern motels in the town. Spotless standard units, some with spa and balcony.

$$$-$$ The Gables, 20 Waikawa Rd, T03-573 6772, thegables.co.nz. Good value with 3 rooms and 2 self-contained cottages.

Motor parks
$$$-$ Blue Anchor Top Ten Holiday Park, 78 Waikawa Rd, T0800-277444, pictontop10.co.nz. An excellent award-winning holiday park. It is well located within walking distance of the town, has tidy cabins and tourist flats and great facilities. It gets crowded, especially if you're camping, so arrive early.

$$-$ Alexanders Holiday Park, Canterbury St, Picton T0800-4742866, T03-5736378, alexanderspicton.co.nz. If the **Blue Anchor** is busy, or you want a more peaceful (but older) site try **Alexanders Holiday Park** on the southern edge of town. It has plenty more space and great (but older) camp kitchen facilities.

Blenheim and the Marlborough vineyards *p56, map p57*
$$$$ Hotel D'Urville, 52 Queen St, Blenheim, T03-577 9945, durville.co.nz. Quality boutique hotel in a former bank in the heart of the town centre. Award-winning restaurant attached.

$$ Cranbrook Cottage, Giffords Rd, Blenheim, T03-572 8606, cranbrook.co.nz. Without doubt one of the most characterful self-contained cottage B&Bs in the region. Set among the vines and fruit trees, the 135-year-old renovated cottage provides plenty of privacy. Breakfast delivered to the door each morning.

$$ St Leonards, 18 St Leonards Rd,
Blenheim, T03-577 8328, stleonards.co.nz.
Beautifully appointed self-contained
accommodation sleeping up to 6, in 3
vineyard cottages (one of which is a former
stables) and a homestead annexe. Open fires,
potbelly stoves and claw-foot baths add to a
cosy, homely atmosphere. Great value.
$ Chartridge Park, SH6 (3 km south of
Havelock), T03-5742129. A superb peaceful
and low-key little motor park with 2 great-
value cabins and a bunkroom. Small camp
kitchen and games lounge with TV.

⊖ Restaurants

Picton *p55, map p55*
$$ Le Café, London Quay, T03-573 5588.
Daily for breakfast, lunch and dinner. Perhaps
the best bet, it has a good atmosphere and
is well placed on the waterfront.

**Blenheim and the Marlborough
vineyards** *p56, map p57*
$$$ Hotel D'Urville, 52 Queen St,
Blenheim, T03-577 9945. Daily 0600-2400.
The place for fine dining in Blenheim itself.
$$$-$$ Herzog, 81 Jeffries Rd, Wairau
Valley, T03-572 8770, herzog.co.nz. Daily,
lunch from 1200-1500 and dinner from 1800.
Just one of many fine winery restaurants.
$$ Raupo Riverside Café, 2 Symonds St,
Blenheim, T03-577 8822. Daily 0730-1900.
Eco-oriented and located on the banks of
the Taylor River in the heart of Blenheim.
$$ The Cork and Keg, Inkerman St,
Renwick, T03-572 9328. Sick of vineyards?
Try this character English-style pub and
brewery with its all-day pub-grub menu.
$$ The Mussel Pot Restaurant,
73 Main Rd, Havelock North, T03-
574 2824, themusselpot.co.nz.
Daily 1000-1500 and from 1730 till
late. Great mussels and chowder.

⊛ Festivals

Marlborough Sounds *p55*
2nd Sat in Feb Marlborough Wine
Festival, T0800-000575, bmw-wine
marlborough-festival.co.nz. A lively
celebration of the region's gourmet
food and wines. Live music provided.

● What to do

Picton *p55, map p55*
Cruises
Beachcomber Fun Cruises, London
Quay, T03-573 6175, T0800-624526,
beachcombercruises.co.nz, and **Endeavour
Express**, based in both Endeavour Inlet
and at the Waterfront in Picton, T03-573
5456, boatrides.co.nz. Wide-ranging cruise
services and packages.
Soundsair, T0800-505005, soundsair.com.
Extraordinary number of flight-seeing
combinations and options that include
one night's lodging, lunch, day walks and
cruises from $150-400.
Sounds Connection, T03-573 8843,
soundsconnection.co.nz. Another
alternative based in Picton.

Tour operators
The Cougar Line, London Quay, T0800-
504090, T03-573 7925, queencharlottetrack.
co.nz. One-way transfers, multi-day walk
packages; mountain-biking packages and
a daily 'Track Pass' that will drop you off at
Ship Cove and pick up at Anakiwa, from
$95. Offers half- or full-day cruise walks
from $55.
Dolphin Watch Ecotours, Picton Foreshore,
T03-573 8040, naturetours.co.nz. Offers
a wide range of eco-based tours to Ship
Cove and Motuara Island Bird Sanctuary
above and beyond its conventional dolphin
swimming and viewing trips.
**Marlborough Sounds Adventure
Company**, London Quay, T03-573 6078.
Guided and self-guided walks of the Queen
Charlotte Track. It also offers kayaking trips

and a 3-day walk/paddle/mountain bike adventure from $585.

Blenheim *p56, map p57*
Wine tours
Marlborough Wine Tours, T03-578 9515, marlboroughwinetours.co.nz. Tour of up to 8 wineries. Flexible itinerary depending on taste, from $43-$79. UK wine-delivery service.
Wine-Tours-By-Bike, T03-577 6954 winetoursbybike.co.nz. This is the common-sense method of visiting the wineries by bike. Half day from $40, full $55, guided tour $25 per hr.

⊖ Transport

Picton *p55, map p55*
Picton offers air and nationwide bus services including Golden bay and the West Coast. The main i-SITES can assist with bookings.

Air
There are flights to **Wellington** with **Soundsair**, T03-520 3080/T0800-505005, soundsair.com, 8 times daily, from $89 one-way.

Boat
For ferry crossings to **North Island** see page 9. The **Interislander** and **Bluebridge** ferries dock at the ferry terminal in Picton 500 m north of the town centre.

Bus
There are many bus companies that serve Picton to/from the south or west including **Intercity**, T03-520 3113/T03-573 7025, intercitycoach.co.nz. Buses drop off or pick up at the railway station, ferry terminal or outside the i-SITE visitor centre. The main booking agent is the i-SITE visitor centre.

Train
The Picton train station on Auckland Stand is the terminus for the daily Coastal Pacific service to/from **Christchurch**, T03-573 8857/T0800-872467, 0900-1700, tranzscenic.co.nz. It arrives daily at 1213 and departs at 1300, from $59-100. This trip is famous for its coastal scenery.

❸ Directory

Picton *p55, map p55*
ATM There are ATMs at the Ferry Terminal and in all the main centres.

Nelson and around

Nelson is known as the sunniest place in the country and one of the most desirable places to live. It is lively and modern, yet steeped in history, its people unpretentious thanks to a large contingent of artisans. Surrounding it, all within 100 km, are some of the most beautiful coastal areas and beaches in New Zealand, not to mention three diverse and stunning national parks, where you can experience some of the most exciting tramping tracks in the South Island, plus a host of other activities. Little wonder then that the Nelson region is one of the top holiday destinations in the country.

Arriving in Nelson

Tourist information
i-SITE visitor centre ① *corner of Trafalgar and Halifax streets, T03-548 2304, nelsonnz.com, Mon-Fri 0830-1700, Sat-Sun 0900-1600.*

Places in Nelson

Civic Tower
There is one sight that must be mentioned straight away, if not out of despair, then in order to highlight that nature-made versus man-made issue mentioned throughout this book. Have you ever seen a building as ugly as Nelson's Civic Tower – across the road from the visitor information centre – you can't miss it? Is that not, without doubt, the most hideous-looking building you have ever seen beyond a public convenience? An utter mess of concrete and steel, covered with aerials and radar. Even the pigeons boycott that one. Enough said.

Nelson Christ Church Cathedral
① *Daily in summer 0800-1900, winter 0800-1700, tours available and entry by donation.*
Although Nelson was one of New Zealand's earliest and largest settlements, there is little architectural evidence. Of obvious notoriety, but hardly historical (having being finally completed in 1965), is the Nelson Christ Church Cathedral. Dominating the southern end of town it has an intriguing almost strangely unconventional design and contains some fine stained-glass windows and a 2000-pipe organ.

Nelson Provincial Museum
① *Corner Hardy and Trafalgar streets, T03-548 9588, museumnp.org.nz. Exhibitions Mon-Fri 1000-1700, Sat-Sun 1000-1630, $7, child $3.*
For the best sense of history head for the Nelson Provincial Museum, which serves as the region's principal museum and contains all the usual suspects covering life from Maori settlement to the present day using an imaginative and dynamic range of well-presented displays.

Nelson galleries

With over 300 artists resident in the town arts and crafts feature heavily in the list of attractions. A copy of the *Nelson Art Guide* is a great memento in itself and available from most bookshops. The **Te Aratoi-o-Whakatu or Suter Gallery** ① *208 Bridge St, T03-548 4699, thesuter.org.nz, daily 1030-1630, $3, child 50c*, heads the list of major art galleries.

Nelson

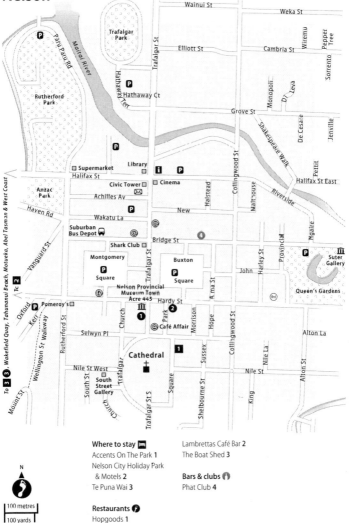

Where to stay 🛏
Accents On The Park **1**
Nelson City Holiday Park
& Motels **2**
Te Puna Wai **3**

Restaurants 🍴
Hopgoods **1**

Lambrettas Café Bar **2**
The Boat Shed **3**

Bars & clubs 🍸
Phat Club **4**

N

100 metres
100 yards

Located next to Queen's Gardens, it boasts four exhibition spaces that showcase both permanent and temporary historical and contemporary collections. There is also a café, cinema and theatre on site that runs a programme of musical and theatrical performances.

There are many other galleries in the area displaying a vast array of creative talent. Of particular note is **Höglund Art Glass** ① *Korurangi Farm, Landsdowne Rd, Richmond, a 20-min drive from Nelson, T03-544 6500, hoglund.co.nz, daily 1000-1700,* home to the Hoglund Glass Blowing Studio. Here the internationally renowned pieces are created for sale and show in the gallery. There is also glassblowing, guided studio tours and a café and the entire set-up is located in a pleasant park-like environment. Also worth a visit is the **South Street Gallery** ① *10 Nile St West, T03-548 8117, nelsonpottery.co.nz.* This is the historical home of the Nelson Pottery where 25 selected potters of national and international renown create their various wares. The street itself is also noted for its 16 working-class historical cottages built between 1863 and 1867.

Around Nelson

World of Wearable Art and Collectable Cars
① *95 Quarantine Rd, Annesbrook, just north of the airport, T03-547 4573, wowcars.co.nz, daily 1000-1830, 1700 in winter, from $22, child $8.*
Set in a 1-ha site the most lauded tourist attraction in the Nelson area has two galleries. The first is the Wearable Art Gallery showcasing the historic Wearable Art Garment collection. There is a fully scripted show that uses mannequins rather than live models but with all the usual elements of sound and lighting. The original concept was first initiated in 1987 as a gallery promotion by local sculptor Suzie Moncrieff and is easy to describe. Choose a theme, make the most remarkable and creative costume imaginable, from any material or media and get a bonny lass to show it off. But such a basic description could never do justice to the results, the story of how it all came about, or, indeed, how it has all developed since – you just have to see it for yourself. This is a remarkable synergy of art and fashion and a true tribute to the creative imagination.

The second gallery has an impressive collection of classic cars formerly on view in the town centre.

Tahunanui Beach and Rabbit Island
Upon arrival you might think for a region famous for its beaches Nelson lets the side down and is bereft of one, but it isn't. Tahunanui Beach is just a few kilometres southwest of the town centre and is particularly well known for kite-surfing. Slightly further afield (20 km) towards Motueka (SH60) are the beaches and forest swathe of Rabbit Island. This seemingly never-ending beach offers a far quieter and expansive alternative.

Nelson Lakes National Park
The slightly under-rated Nelson Lakes National Park 90 km south of Nelson protects 102,000 ha of the northernmost Southern Alps range. Its long, scenic and trout-filled lakes – Rotoroa and Rotoiti – cradled in beech-clad alpine ranges, hiding beautiful tussock valleys and wildflower-strewn meadows, dominate the park. Although a quick look at the lakes are all that most people see of this park, the ranges and river valleys offer some superb walking. The two most noted tramps are the 80-km, four- to seven-day Traverse-Sabine Circuit and the excellent two- to three-day Robert Ridge/Lake Angelus Track. There are a number of very pleasant short walks from 20 minutes to two hours that extend into the park from St Arnaud

or Lake Rotoroa. The principal base for the park is the pretty village of **St Arnaud**, which nestles at the northern end of Lake Rotoiti. Almost all accommodation, services, major park access and activities are located here including the **DoC Nelson Lakes National Park visitor centre** ① *T03-5211806, doc.govt.nz, daily 0800-1900 seasonal*, providing comprehensive displays and information, as well as offering advice on local accommodation and water taxi transport.

Murchison

A further 65 km along SH6 from St Arnaud delivers you in Murchison at the head of the Buller Gorge and junction of the Matakitaki and Buller rivers. It is a service centre for the local farming community and for many, the gateway to the west coast from the north. Although once an important gold-mining town (and famous for being nearly wiped out by a violent earthquake in 1929), it is today a quiet place, primarily of interest to the tourist as the base for a number of interesting activities including rafting and kayaking. It is also the haunt of the odd serious tramper intent on exploring the remote southern wilderness of the Kahurangi National Park.

Nelson to Motueka

From Richmond, 14 km southwest of Nelson, SH60 follows the fringe of Nelson Bay west to Motueka. This route – often labelled as Nelson's Coastal Way – is the realm of vineyards, orchards, arts and crafts outlets and some pleasant seaside spots. One such spot worth a look, particularly around lunch or dinnertime, is Mapua. A congenial little settlement at the mouth of the Waimea Inlet (and just a short diversion off SH60), it has a few interesting art and craft shops, a small aquarium and one of the best restaurants in the region, The Smokehouse, which does good fish and chips.

Wineries are also a big feature in the Nelson Region and particularly the Moutere Valley and although the fine winemakers perhaps suffer from the reputation and sheer scale of their much-hyped neighbours in Marlborough, the wine they produce can be of a very fine quality. For more information on Nelson Region wineries consult the i-SITE visitor centre in Nelson or Motueka for a list of some of the better-known wineries.

Motueka

Motueka itself is a rather unremarkable little place, but set amidst all the sun-bathed vineyards and orchards and within a short distance from some of the most beautiful beaches in the country, it seems to radiate a sense of smug satisfaction. Once a thriving Maori settlement, the first residents were quickly displaced by the early Europeans, who were also intent on utilizing the area's rich natural resources. Today Motueka is principally a service centre for the numerous vineyards, orchards and market gardens that surround it, or for the many transitory tourists on route to the Abel Tasman National Park and Golden Bay. With such a seasonal influx of visitors Motueka is also a place of contrast, bustling in summer and sleepy in winter. One thing you will immediately notice on arrival is its almost ludicrously long main street – so long you could land a 747 on it and still have room for error.

Kaiteriteri and Marahau

Kaiteriteri and Marahau (the gateway to the Abel Tasman National Park) are both accessed from SH60 just north of Motueka. Kaiteriteri (13 km) is a very pretty village with two exquisite beaches of its own and is a popular holiday spot. The main beach is the departure point for scenic launch trips, water taxis and kayak adventures into the park. If you do nothing else in Kaiteriteri, allow yourself time to take in the view from the Kaka Pa Point Lookout at

Day walk: Torrent Bay to Marahau

If you are short of time or cannot stand the sight of a paddle, the following day-walk will provide a pleasant taste to what the Abel Tasman is all about. They are also not too strenuous and have the added fun of getting your feet wet.

Torrent Bay to Marahau: 14 km; three to six hours.

From Marahau take an early morning water taxi to Torrent Bay, $40. Although there is an alternate high-tide route around Torrent Bay – try to make sure your arrival at Torrent Bay coincides with low tide so you can make the direct crossing. Take in the immediate delights here, then take the Coastal Track heading south, for which you need to take off your boots and then follow the markers across the estuary. Return boots to feet and find the track again that climbs the small headland before falling to the exquisite Anchorage Bay Beach. Then, from halfway up the beach, climb the hill, not forgetting to look back at the stunning view. Take the side track (15 minutes) from the top of the hill down to the incredibly cute (and hopefully quiet) Watering Cove. Climb back up to the coastal track and continue south. If you have time, check out Stillwell Bay and certainly walk along Appletree Bay (re-access to main track at the far end of the beach). From there complete the walk past Tinline Bay to the Marahau entrance point. If the tide is in your favour, you can cross the bay directly just beyond Tinline Bay (where the path descends to beach level). Fall exhausted and happy in to the Park Café, reward yourself with a pint of beer, a glass of wine or the full seafood fettuccine.

the eastern end of the beach. There is a signpost with destinations and distances that will remind you how far you are from home – and how close to paradise. Breakers Beach below, looking east towards the park, is truly idyllic – and yes, who does own that house?

Marahau a further 6 km east of Kaiteriteri, is principally an accommodation and activity base at the main access point to the national park. There is a good range of accommodation options, a number of water taxi and activity operators and a café to satisfy the needs of hungry trampers.

Abel Tasman National Park

The Abel Tasman is the smallest national park in New Zealand, and one of the most beautiful, protecting 23,000 ha of some of the finest coastal scenery and beaches in the country. Rolling hills of native bush fall to azure-coloured clear waters and a 91-km coastline, indented with over 50 beaches of golden sand. It is a paradise for trampers and sea kayakers and boasts the famous and increasingly popular 51 km two- to five-day Coastal Walkway. The park is also home to the Tonga Island Marine Reserve – the preserve of all manner of sea life including some friendly and inquisitive fur seals.

Opened in 1942 after the tireless efforts of conservationist and resident Perrine Moncrieff, the park was named after the Dutch navigator Abel Tasman who first sighted New Zealand in 1642. Many of the place names are accredited to the explorations and subsequent mappings in 1827 by the French explorer (and man in possession of an extraordinarily grand name) Jules Sebastian Cesar Dumont d'Urville.

A word of warning: this small stretch of coastline, with its picturesque sandy bays and well-worn coastal walking track is one of the most popular natural attractions in the country. As such, it seldom disappoints, but don't expect to find much solitude here. In summer it can all get a bit silly and the park now attracts four times as many people as it did a decade ago (now 120,000)!

Other than the obvious waterborne sightseeing trips the various services and schedules offer casual walkers or day-trippers the option of being dropped off at one beach to be picked up later at the same, or at another. For trampers this can also provide numerous options to walk some or all of the Coastal Walkway. Note also that some operators will tow kayaks, giving you the option to kayak, walk or indeed retire from the track early. Bags and backpacks can also be carried independently, but this tends to be in conjunction with organized trips. The choice and combinations are vast, so study what is available prior to your arrival. The **Motueka i-SITE** ① *Wallace St, in the town centre, T03-528 6543, abeltasmangreenrush.co.nz, daily 0800-1800/0800-1630 winter*, provides the best, most up-to-date and most importantly, non-biased information on the park. The **DoC visitor centre** ① *Nelson T03-546 9339*, or the **field centre** ① *Motueka, corner of King Edward and High streets, T03-528 1810, doc.govt.nz, Mon-Fri 0800-1630*, has maps and leaflets for the entire region and can book huts for the Abel Tasman Coastal Walkway. You could also call into **Abel Tasman Wilson's Experiences** ① *265 High St, T03-528 2027/0800-223582, abeltasmanco.nz*, which operates beachfront lodges, launch cruises, water taxi, guided/non-guided sea kayaking and walking; it can provide maps, tide information and help with itinerary planning.

Nelson and around listings

For hotel and restaurant price codes and other relevant information, see pages 9-13.

☺ Where to stay

Nelson *p62, map p63*
$$$$-$$$ Te Puna Wai, 24 Richardson St, Port Hills, T03-548 7621, tepunawai.co.nz. An immaculate villa-style B&B set overlooking the bay in the Port Hills area. Three luxury en suite rooms, 2 of which can be combined to form a spacious apartment. Great views, open fire, classy decor and hosts that go the extra mile.
$$-$ Accents on the Park, 335 Trafalgar Sq, T03-548 4335, trafalgaraccommodation. co.nz. In a word: exceptional. A beautifully renovated Victorian villa with a distinct air of class. A full range of well-appointed rooms from en suite to shared dorms with all the usual facilities and a lovingly constructed basement lounge bar with open fire and plenty of character.
$$-$ Nelson City Holiday Park & Motels, 230 Vanguard St, T03-548 1445, nelsonholidaypark.co.nz. Closest quality

park to the city centre. Full range of units and cabins, powered sites, camp kitchen.

Nelson to Motueka *p65*
$$$$ Jester House, 15 km south of Motueka on the Coastal Highway (SH60), T03-526 6742, jesterhouse.co.nz. Something totally different and without doubt the most original accommodation in the region. Quite simply, this could be (and probably will be) your only opportunity to stay in a giant boot.
$$$ Rowan Cottage Organic B&B, 27 Fearon St, T03-528 6492, rowancottage. net. Studio with good facilities and character amidst a proudly nurtured organic garden.

Motor parks
$$$-$ Mapua Leisure Park, 33 Toru St, T03-540 2666, nelson holiday.co.nz. An excellent camp, set amidst pine trees and sheltered surroundings, at the river mouth. It has numerous pretty areas to camp in, powered sites, cabins, chalets, sauna, pool and spa. There is also a small café and bar on the beach and internet.

Kaiteriteri and Marahau *p65*

$$$ Abel Tasman National Park Torrent Bay Lodge, T03-528 7801, abeltasman. co.nz. Owned and operated by Abel Tasman Wilson's Experiences offer an excellent standard of modern, mid- to upper-range accommodation as part of a walks or kayaking package from 2 days/1 night to 5 days/4 nights.

$$$-$$ Abel Tasman Ocean View Chalets, 305 Sandy Bay Marahau Rd, T03-527 8232, accommodationabeltasman.co.nz. Neat, self-contained 1- to 2-bedroom cottages and studio units set on the hillside overlooking the bay, about 500 m from the main village.

$$$-$ Old McDonald's Farm and Holiday Park, Harvey Rd, at the entrance to the Abel Tasman Park, T03-527 8288, old macs.co.nz. A large but sheltered, well-facilitated holiday camp complete with various animals, including 2 friendly and extremely dozy kune pigs. There are plenty of sheltered tent and powered sites and a range of well-appointed self-contained units, cabins and a backpacker's dormitory. Small café and shop on site and internet. Within walking distance of the Park Café.

🍴 Restaurants

Nelson *p62, map p63*

$$$ Hopgoods Restaurant and Bar, 284 Trafalgar St, T03-545 7191. Quality locally sourced cuisine, with much of it organic.

$$$ The Boat Shed, 350 Wakefield Quay, T03-546 9783, theboatshedcafe.co.nz. Daily for breakfast, lunch and dinner. Fresh, local seafood a speciality.

$$ Lambrettas Café Bar, 204 Hardy St, T03-545 8555, lambrettascafe.co.nz. Open 0900-late. A popular, good value café specializing in all things Italian.

Nelson to Motueka *p65*

$$ The Smokehouse Café, Mapua, T03-540 2280, smokehouse.co.nz. Daily for lunch and dinner. Known for its smoked fish. Also has takeaway fish and chips.

Motueka *p65*

$$ Hot Mamma's Café and Bar, 105 High St, T03-528 7039. Sun-Thu 0900-2200, Fri/Sat 0900-0100. Good licensed café and in the evening a good vibe with musos.

Kaiteriteri and Marahau *p65*

$$ Park Café, Harvey Rd, Marahau, T03-527 8270. Daily from 0800 (closed May-Aug). Just at the southern (main) entrance to the park. Fine blackboard fare, a bar, good coffee and internet.

✺ Festivals

Nelson *p62, map p63*
2nd Sat in Feb Nelson Arts Festival, a week-long celebration showcasing many forms of artistic expression.

◯ Shopping

Nelson *p62, map p63*
Nelson Market, Montgomery Sq. Every Sat, 0800-1300. Local arts and crafts.

◐ What to do

Nelson *p62, map p63*
Adventure activities
Happy Valley Adventures, 194 Cable Bay Rd, Nelson, T03-545 0304, happyvalley adventures.co.nz. Back-country guided quad bike rides, taking in some superb views. Interesting eco-based commentary. An excellent wet weather option. From 1-4 hrs $85-160, standard tour $95 for 2½ hrs. Also Skywire a 4-person flying-fox that runs 1.6 km across the valley, reputedly at 120 kph, from $85. Transportation available.

Climbing
Vertical Limits, 34 Vanguard St, T03-545 7511, verticallimits.co.nz. Open Mon-Thu 1200-2100, Fri-Sun 1200-1800. Offers some excellent half- or full-day rock-climbing trips to some notable venues in Golden Bay, $75-150. Tandem paragliding

is another option. It also has a climbing wall, from $16.

Handicrafts
Creative Tourism, T03-526 8812, creative tourism.co.nz. From $32 you can try your hand at a range of contemporary or traditional crafts from bone carving to organic brewing.

Kitesurfing
Kitescool, T021-354 837, kitescool.co.nz. Kitesurfing is huge in Nelson with the winds over Tahunanui Beach often creating the perfect conditions. Lessons from $150.

Tour operators
Bay Tours, 48 Brougham St, T03-548 6486, baytoursnelson.co.nz. Flexible with wine and art tours a speciality, from $89.

Motueka *p65*
Aerial activities
Skydive Abel Tasman, Motueka Airfield, 16 College St, T03-528 4091, T0800-422899, skydive.co.nz. If the weather is in your favour you can do a tandem skydive from 9000 ft ($249).
Tasman Bay Air Nelson, T03-528 8290, flytasmanbay.co.nz. Flights across both Kahurangi and Abel Tasman National Parks. A truly memorable experience.
U-Fly Extreme, Motueka Airfield, College St, T03-528 8290, T0800-360180, uflyextreme. co.nz. Fun to the extreme aboard a Pitts-Special Biplane. A once-in-a-lifetime opportunity to actually fly an aerobatic aircraft yourself, from $299 (15-min flight). Remarkably easy, safe, good value for money.

Tour operators
Abel Tasman Wilson's Experiences, 265 High St, T0800-223582, T03-528 2027, abeltasmanco.nz. Operates beachfront lodges, launch cruises, water taxi, guided/non-guided sea kayaking and walking; it can provide maps, tide information and help with itinerary planning.

Kaiteriteri and Marahau *p65*
Kayaking
Kahu Kayaks, Sandy Bay Rd, Marahau, T03-527 8300, T0800-300101, kahukayaks.co.nz. One of many companies based around the southern section of the park. Good local knowledge, but compare prices and options. Freedom rentals available.

Tour operators
Abel Tasman Aqua Taxi, Marahau, T03-527 8083, T0800-278282, aquataxis.co.nz. Has an office and café (where you also board your boat). Prices are reasonable and competitive. An average fare to Totaranui at the top end of the park will cost from $40 one-way. Most water taxis depart between 0830 and 1030 from Motueka, Kaiteriteri and Marahau with additional sailings in the early afternoon (1200 and 1330), depending on the tides.

⊖ Transport

Nelson *p62, map p63*
Air
Nelson airport serves the main national centres.

Bus
Buses to and throughout the Nelson region, including the **Abel Tasman National Park**, can be booked at the Nelson i-SITE visitor centre.

ⓘ Directory

Nelson *p62, map p63*
Hospital Nelson Hospital, Tipahi St, T03-546 1800. **Pharmacy** Emergency pharmacy, corner of Hardy and Collingwood streets, T03-548 3897.

Golden Bay

Beyond Motueka SH60 makes the steep ascent of Takaka Hill to the quieter, far more laid-back realms of Golden Bay. Beyond the great hill, the small arty township of Takaka offers a fine introduction to the region, while the nearby Pupu Springs possess an almost palpable sense of peace, and an extraordinary clarity. Then, skirting the shores of Golden Bay, via the former gold rush town of Collingwood, SH60 finally terminates at the surreal sandy sweep of Farewell Spit, with the unforgettable beauty of Wharariki Beach within walking distance. All in all, it can prove a memorable diversion and the scenery and general atmosphere of this little corner of the South Island can act like a natural tranquillizer from the people overload experienced around the Abel Tasman National Park.

Takaka

Takaka was founded in 1854 and is the principal business and shopping area for Golden Bay. In summer it is a bustling little place and year round the residence of a colourful and cosmopolitan palette of arts and crafts people. There are a number of interesting attractions around the town including Pupu Springs and Rawhiti Cave. The township also serves as the gateway to the northern sector of the Abel Tasman National Park. **i-SITE visitor centre** ① *Willow St, Takaka, Golden Bay, T03-525 9136.*

The biggest attraction in the immediate area are the beautiful and crystal-clear **Te Waikoropupu** or **Pupu Springs** administered by DoC. (north of Takaka left off SH60). Borne of the Takaka Marble Aquifer, the turquoise waters of the 'Pupu Springs' bubbles out at an average rate of 13.2 cu m per second, creating a lake that is the clearest of any freshwater body outside Antarctica. To the Maori, the springs are considered taonga – a treasure, and wahi tapu – a sacred place to be revered. It is a peaceful, beautiful place that has a palpable and rare sense of purity lost in the parks and reserves in the more populous nations of the world.

Also close to Takaka are the weird and wonderful limestone (karst) formations of the **Labyrinth Rocks** ① *3 km outside town, Labyrinth Lane, Three Oaks, T03-5258434, daily 1200-dusk, $7.* It is not a cave system so is great for kids.

Also worth a day of exploration is the **Totaranui Road** via the beachside village of Pohara, Wainui Bay and the Northern sector of the Abel Tasman National Park. Features along the way include the Abel Tasman Memorial on the headland just beyond Tarakohe, the Wainui Falls (an easy 40 min walk) and of course Totaranui itself with its picture postcard orange sand!

Bencarri Farm ① *6 km south of Takaka, signposted off SH60 on McCallum Rd, T03-525 8261, bencarri.co.nz, daily 1000-1730, $12, child $6,* is something of a novelty with its tame eels – yes, eels – reputed to be the oldest in the country with some individuals still enjoying a daily snack after 80 years of residence. Bencarri Farm also has a host of more congenial touchy-feely animals including llamas and some homesick Scottish 'Heelaan coos'. There is a good café on site (open 1000-late).

Collingwood

Collingwood was formerly known as Gibbstown and was (believe it or not) once a booming gold-mining town that was promoted as an eminently suitable capital for the nation. But that dream turned to dust when the gold reserves were laid waste and a fire almost destroyed the entire village. Rebuilt and renamed Collingwood in honour of Nelson's second-in-command, fire struck again in 1904 and yet again as recently as 1967 when the town hall, hotel and two shops were reduced to ashes. Despite its fiery past, Collingwood still retains a few historical buildings, including the former courthouse, which is now a café where you can sentence yourself to a lengthy tea break.

South of Collingwood, in the attractive Aorere River Valley and back on the limestone theme, are the privately owned **Te Anaroa** and **Rebecca Caves** ① *Caves Rd, near Rockville, T03-524 8131, teanaroacaves.co.nz, 1-hr guided tours of the Te Anaroa Caves available, $20, child $10; dual cave tours of 3½ hrs are also available.* The Te Anaroa Caves are 350 m in length and include the usual stalactite and stalagmite formations and fossilized shells, while the Rebecca Caves are best known for their glow-worms. At the end of Cave Road are two limestone rock monoliths known as the Devil's Boots (presumably because they are upside-down).

Farewell Spit

Access on the spit is restricted so an organized tour is the only way to truly experience this weird and wonderful place. You can also book and join the Farewell Spit tour en route to the spit at the visitor centre, or see tour operators, page 74.

The spit, which is only around 20 m at its highest, is formed entirely from countless tons of sand ejected into the northerly ocean currents from the numerous rivermouths scattered all the way up the west coast. Both Cape Farewell and Farewell Spit were noted by Tasman in 1642 (no doubt a little shorter than it is now) and named by Cook when he left the shores of New Zealand in 1770. It is a dynamic, almost desert-like landscape, with sparse vegetation struggling to take root in the dry and constantly shifting sand. The majority of the spit is a DoC nature reserve and the vast mud flats that it creates along its landward edge are one of New Zealand's most important wading-bird habitats. Over 100 species have been recorded around the spit, with some migrating flocks of well in to the thousands, providing a memorable sight. Hundreds of black swans also use the food-rich mud flats of Golden Bay, and there is also a small colony of rapacious gannets at the very end of the spit.

The lighthouse, at the very tip of the spit, was first erected in 1870. It has an interesting history and was replaced due to rotting timber.

At the base of the spit and just beyond the last small settlement of Puponga is the **Farewell Spit Visitor Centre** ① *T03-5248454, daily 0900-1700*. It stocks a range of leaflets and has a number of displays surrounding the spit, its wildlife and the rather sad and repetitive whale strandings in Golden Bay. The café sells a range of refreshments and snacks and has a deck overlooking the bay and the spit itself. Most of the established walking tracks leave directly from the centre.

Whariki Beach

Whariki Beach has to be one of the most beautiful beaches in the country. Perhaps it is its very remoteness that makes it so special, but add to that its classic features – including caves, arches and dunes – and you have near perfection. It is so beautiful you almost find yourself feeling a corrupting sense of guilt at leaving your lone footprints on its swathes of golden sand. You can access the beach by road from Puponga via Whariki Road (20-minute walk) or make it the highlight on a longer and stunning coastal walk from Pillar Point Lighthouse. Note that swimming here is very dangerous. Horse treks to and on the beach are also available.

If you cannot afford to go out on the spit and do not have time to walk to Whariki Beach, or simply want to get a better impression of its scale from afar, the best place to view it is from the elevated hills around the Pillar Point Light Beacon, accessed by foot from Whariki Road and Puponga.

Kahurangi National Park

Kahurangi is New Zealand's second largest national park, after Fiordland. It is a vast and remote landscape of rugged alpine ranges and river valleys, the most notable being the Heaphy, which meets, in part, the park's most famous tramping route, the **Heaphy Track**. One of the most interesting features of the park is its ancient geology. It contains some of the country's oldest rock landforms, with spectacular limestone caves, plateau, arches and outcrops. Kahurangi is home to over half of New Zealand's native plant species (over 80%

Day walk: Pillar Point to Whariariki Beach coastal walk

Pillar Point to Whariariki Beach: 13 km; six to eight hours.

From Puponga, follow Whariariki Beach Road to the turn-off (right) up to Pillar Point Light Beacon ('Blinking Billy'). Note this is a rough non-signposted road. Park your vehicle at the base of the hill below the light beacon. Climb the hill to Pillar Point and enjoy your first proper view of Farewell Spit before heading further north towards the Old Man Rock (155 m) along the crest of the hill. Take in the views of the spit and Golden Bay before retracing your steps to Pillar Point. From Pillar Point follow the sporadic orange markers south through a small tract of manuka trees. From there follow the markers and the cliffs taking in all the cliff-top views to Cape Farewell. Keep your eyes peeled for fur seals, whose plaintive cries will probably reach the senses first. Continue south along the cliffs before descending to Whariariki Beach. If the tide is in your favour, walk its entire length and investigate the many caves and rock corridors along its length. Once at the base of Pilch Point (at the very end of all the beaches) retrace your steps to Pillar Point.

of all alpine species) and over 18 native bird species, including the New Zealand falcon, the great spotted kiwi and the huge New Zealand land snail.

The low-level 82-km Heaphy Track takes four to six days and is noted for its diverse habitats, open areas and beautiful coastal scenery (western end). It is usually negotiated from west to east and the western trailhead starts about 15 km north of Karamea, while the eastern, starts 28 km south of Collingwood. Take insect repellent with you.

For information on the park and its tramping tracks consult the DoC or i-SITES in Nelson, Motueka or Takaka.

Golden Bay listings

For hotel and restaurant price codes and other relevant information, see pages 9-13.

● Where to stay

Takaka *p71*
Motor parks
$$$-$ Pohara Beach Top Ten Holiday Park and Motels, Abel Tasman Dr, Pohara, T03-525 9500, pohara.com/paradise. The best motor camp with tent, powered sites, modern timber kitchen cabins and full facilities all next to the beach, 10 km north of Takaka.

Collingwod *p71*
$$$-$$ Adrift, 10 km south of Collingwod, 52 Tukurua Rd, Tukurua, T03-525 8353, accommodationgoldenbay.com. Excellent self-contained, beachside luxury cottages, designed for 2 but accommodating 3. Plenty of privacy, beautiful surroundings and great hosts.

Farewell Spit *p72*
$$ Innlet and Cottages, Main Rd, Pakawau, on the road to Farewell Spit, T03-524 8040, goldenbayindex.co.nz/theinnlet. Oozes character and is in a lovely bush setting offering dorms, twins and doubles and charming self-contained cottages, studio apartment and a flat that sleep 3-6. Bike hire available and excellent harbour/rainforest kayak trips, guided or self-guided. Internet.

● Restaurants

Takaka *p71*
$$$-$$ Mussel Inn, Onekaka, half way between Takaka and Collingwood on SH60, T03-525 9241, musselinn.co.nz. Open 1100-late. Good pub grub with great-value mussels and good beer.

$$ Wholemeal Café, Commercial St, T03-525 9426, wholemealcafe.co.nz. Daily 0730-late. Good coffee, breakfasts, health-conscious blackboard menu and excellent service.

Collingwod *p71*
$$ Courthouse Café, corner of Gibbs and Elizabeth streets, T03-5248025. Daily 0830-late (seasonal). Sentence yourself to tea and scones at this former courthouse.

● Shopping

Takaka *p71*
Golden Bay Museum and Gallery, T03-525 6268. Daily 1000-1600, closed Sun in winter, $1. Showcases the cream of local arts and crafts talent.

● What to do

Abel Tasman National Park *p66*
Kayaking
Golden Bay Kayaks, Pohara, Golden Bay, T03-525 9095, goldenbaykayaks.co.nz. Popular and slightly different with trips in both the Abel Tasman National Park and Golden Bay region.

Farewell Spit *p72*
Horse riding
Cape Farewell Horse Treks, Puponga, T03-524 8031, horsetreksnz.com. Some of the most scenic routes in the country, including Wharariki Beach (3 hrs, $130).

Tour operators
Farewell Spit Tours, 6 Tasman St, T03-524 8257, T0800-808257, farewellspit.com. This is, as the name suggests, the original tour operator and has been taking people out on to the spit for over 60 years. Range of themed eco-oriented options lasting 6½ hrs.

Contents

Footprint features

Otago & Southland

Dunedin and Otago Peninsula

There is perhaps nowhere else in the world – and certainly nowhere so far from its roots – that boasts a Scottish heritage like Dunedin, the South Island's second largest city. A city born of Scottish immigrants who arrived in 1848 even the name means 'Edin on the Hill' after Edinburgh, the Scottish capital. The streets are also blatant in their similarity, sharing the names of Edinburgh's most famous, including Princes Street and George Street.

Immediately, you will also notice the echo of Scottish architecture – grand buildings of stone, built to last, which go far beyond the merely functional and, in true Scottish tradition, defy inclement weather. Most were built during the great Otago gold boom of the 1860s when the city enjoyed considerable prosperity and standing.

Modern-day Dunedin has many tourism assets, of which the Otago Peninsula is perhaps the best known. Dunedin's 'beautiful backyard' (as it is often called) is home to some rare wildlife including the only mainland breeding colony of albatross, the rare yellow-eyed penguins and Hooker's sea lions. There is also one other undeniable asset to Dunedin, and one that can perhaps be attributed to its Scots heritage: without doubt it has the friendliest people and offers the warmest welcome in New Zealand.

Arriving in Dunedin

Getting there

Dunedin International Airport ① *T03-4862879, dnairport.co.nz*, is 27 km south of the city. Several companies offer airport shuttles including **Super Shuttles** ① *T0800-748885, supershuttle.co.nz*. Expect to pay from $20 for the shuttle and $60 for a taxi (one way). **City Taxis** ① *T0800-771771*; **Dunedin Taxis** ① *T03-477 7777*. Most regional bus companies heading north or south stop at the airport. Regional buses arrive and depart from **Ritchies/InterCity Travel** ① *205 St Andrew St, T03-4717143*, or from the Railway Station.

Tourist information

Octagon i-SITE visitor centre ① *No 48, below the Municipal Chambers Building, T03-474 3300, dunedinnz.com, cityofdunedin.com, Mon-Fri 0800-1800, Sat-Sun 0845-1800*. Also acts as a transport booking agent.

Places in Dunedin

The Octagon

The Octagon forms the heart or central focus of the city and consists of a circular thoroughfare bisected by the city's main streets; George Street to the northeast of the Octagon and Princes Street to the southwest of it. These two streets form the hub of Dunedin's central business district. Presiding over the Octagon is a statue of **Robert Burns** the Scottish poet, whose nephew, the Reverend Thomas Burns, was a religious leader of the early settlers. There are many fine examples of the city's architecture, including the grand **Municipal Chambers** buildings, which now houses the i-SITE visitor centre. Next door to the Municipal Chambers is **St Paul's Cathedral**, just one of several noted for their robust architectural aesthetics. Others worth seeing are the **First Church of Otago** on Moray Place and **St Joseph's Cathedral** on the corner of Rattray and Smith Street.

The Octagon is also home to the **Dunedin Public Art Gallery** ① *T03-477 4000, dunedin. art.museum.co.nz, daily 1000 1700, free*. It is the oldest art gallery in the country and of special note is its collection of New Zealand works that date from 1860 to the present day. There are also some works by the more familiar names like Turner, Gainsborough and Monet.

The trees in the Octagon are automatically and regularly watered from high up within their canopies and there is no protection afforded to pedestrians below. For the uninitiated, particularly on a cloudless day, it can be quite a spectacle as with no warning it starts to rain. Most say it is a council design blunder, while others reckon it is to remind city residents of their Scots heritage.

South and east of the Octagon

A five-minute walk east of the Octagon is Dunedin's iconic train station – a fine example of the typical Scottish desire to take architecture beyond the purely functional. Built in 1906, its grand towered exterior cannot fail to impress, but the interior too is rather splendid complete with stained-glass windows, Royal Doulton tiles, mosaics and brass fittings. For many years it served as a major hub of transportation south to Invercargill and north to Christchurch and beyond. With the steady decline of rail services in New Zealand it now is largely redundant but for the tourism-based **Taieri Gorge** rail journey (see box, page 80) and the occasional 'steam-up' of working engines from around the country.

On the first floor of the station is the **New Zealand Sports Hall of Fame** ① *T03-477 7775, nzhalloffame.co.nz, daily 1000-1600, from $5, child $2*, which celebrates the legacy of more than a century of New Zealand champions.

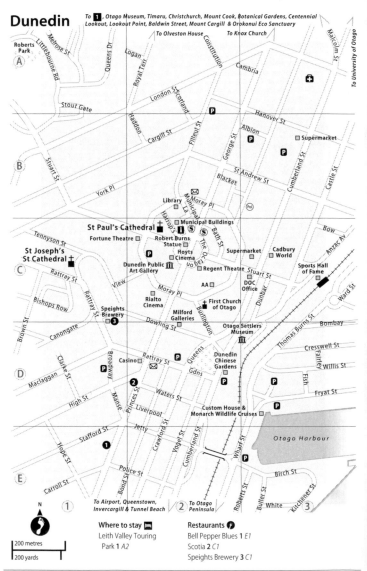

Dunedin

To ■, Otago Museum, Timaru, Christchurch, Mount Cook, Botanical Gardens, Centennial Lookout, Lookout Point, Baldwin Street, Mount Cargill & Orokonui Eco Sanctuary

To University of Otago

Roberts Park

To Olveston House   To Knox Church

Melrose St
Littlebourne Rd
Queens Dr
Logan
Royal Terr
London St
Constitution
Scotland St
Malcolm St

Stout Gate
Haddon
Cambria
Cargill St
Filleul St
Hanover St
George St
Albion
Supermarket
St Andrew St
Cumberland St
Castle St

Stuart St
York Pl
Blacket
Moray Pl
Library
Municipal Buildings

St Paul's Cathedral
Fortune Theatre
Robert Burns Statue
Bath St
The Octagon
Bow

Tennyson St
St Joseph's St Cathedral
Hoyts Cinema
Supermarket
Cadbury World
Anzac Av

Rattray St
View
Dunedin Public Art Gallery
Regent Theatre
Stuart St
Sports Hall of Fame

Bishops Row
Moray Pl
AA
DOC Office
Dunbar
Ward St

Rattray St
Rialto Cinema
First Church of Otago
Bombay

Brown St
Speights Brewery
Milford Galleries
Burlington
Otago Settlers Museum
Thomas Burns St

Canongate
Dowling St
Cresswell St

Maclaggan
Broadway
Casino
Rattray St
Queens
Dunedin Chinese Gardens
Willis St
Fish
Fryat St

Clarke St
Manse
Princes St
Waters St
Custom House & Monarch Wildlife Cruises

High St
Liverpool
Crawford St
Jetty

Stafford St
Vogel St
Cumberland St
Wharf St
Otago Harbour

Hope St
Bond St
Police St
Roberts St
Butler St
White
Birch St
Kitchener St
Carroll St

N

To Airport, Queenstown, Invercargill & Tunnel Beach   To Otago Peninsula

200 metres
200 yards

Where to stay 🛏
Leith Valley Touring
Park **1** A2

Restaurants 🍴
Bell Pepper Blues **1** E1
Scotia **2** C1
Speights Brewery **3** C1

Just a few hundred metres from the train station, and boasting a couple of monstrous historic steam trains of its own, is the **Otago Settlers Museum** ① *31 Queens Gardens, T03-477 5052, otago.settlers.museum.co.nz, closed for redevelopment at the time of research but due to reopen Dec 2012*. First established in 1898 the emphasis here is on social history with many fine temporary and permanent displays. Recent additions include the Across the Ocean Waves exhibit, which focuses on the ocean crossings that many of the early settlers had to endure. The museum also serves as the base for Walk Dunedin, which offers two-hour city heritage walks departing daily at 1000, $20, T03-474 3300.

Next door to the Settlers Museum is the new **Dunedin Chinese Garden** ① *T03-477 3248, chinesegarden.co.nz, daily 1000-1700 and Wed 1900-2100, $9, children free*. Completed in 2008 using authentic Chinese materials crafted by a team of artisans/craftsmen for Dunedin's sister city of Shanghai it is a fine example and a great place to escape the buzz of the city.

North of the railway station is **Cadbury World** ① *280 Cumberland St, T03-4677967/T0800-223287, cadburyworld.co.nz; regular tours 0900-1515, $20, child $13*, which recently opened its doors to the drooling public. Though they could never quite live up to the fantasy of Charlie and the Chocolate Factory the interactive tours offer an interesting and mouth-watering insight into the production of the irresistible stuff. Naturally, there is a shop that does very well.

Dunedin has its own **surf beach** fringing the suburb of **St Claire** (2.5 km) where it is not entirely unusual to see fur seals playing up with the surfers. **Tunnel Beach** is also a popular spot and a precursor to the splendid coastal scenery of the Otago Peninsula. A steep path through some bush delivers you to some impressive weathered sandstone cliffs and arches. Beach access is south of the city centre near Blackhead, 1 km, one hour return; car park seaward end of Green Island Bush Road off Blackhead Road.

North and west of the Octagon

About 1 km north of the Octagon, is the 1906 'Edwardian time capsule' of **Olveston House** ① *42 Royal Terr, T03-4773320, olveston.co.nz; guided 1-hr tours recommended, $17, child $8* Bequeathed to the city in 1966 by the last surviving member of the wealthy and much-travelled Theomin family, the 35-room mansion comes complete with an impressive 'collection of collections', containing many items from the Edwardian era. It gives an interesting insight into Dunedin of old and the lives of the more prosperous pioneer.

A few minutes' east of Olveston, the **Otago Museum** ① *419 Great King St, T03-474 7474, otagomuseum.govt.nz, daily 1000-1700, free; 'Discovery World' $10, child $5; guided tours daily at 1130, $12*, was established in 1868 and is one of the oldest in the country, with a staggering 1.7 million items. The museum's primary themes are culture, nature and science, all housed in newly renovated surroundings and displayed in the now almost obligatory state-of-the-art fashion. The Southern Land, Southern People exhibit is particularly good and is intended to reflect the unique beauty and diversity of Southern New Zealand. The latest edition to the permanent exhibits is **Discovery World Tropical Forest – Live Butterfly Experience**, featuring around 1000 imported tropical butterflies. The museum has a café on site.

A short stroll from the museum is the sprawling campus of the **University of Otago**. Founded in 1869, it was New Zealand's first university and is famous for its architecture as well as its contributions to medical science. The grand edifice of the original Administration building and clock tower (access from Leith St) is perhaps the most photographed icon in the city.

Another New Zealand 'first' in Dunedin are the **Botanical Gardens** ① *T03-4774000, dawn to dusk*, north of the university campus, corner of Great King Street and Opoho Road.

Taieri Gorge Railway and the Otago Central Rail Trail

The Taieri Gorge Railway is considered a world-class train trip encompassing the scenic splendour and history of Otago's hinterland. The former goldfields supply line was completed in 1891 and, as one negotiates the Taieri Gorge with the aid of 12 viaducts and numerous tunnels, it very quickly becomes apparent why it took over 12 years to build. The four-hour trip gets off to a fine start amidst the splendour of Dunedin's grand train station before heading inland to the gorge and Pukerangi. An informative commentary is provided along the way and you are allowed to disembark at certain points of interest. Also, if you ask really nicely, you may also be able to ride alongside the locomotive engineer.

Details available at the train station or T03-477 4449, taieri.co.nz. Trips to Pukerangi/Middlemarch depart daily October-April at 1430 (additional trip on Friday and Sunday at 0930), Pukerangi $86 return; extended trip to Middlemarch $99. Licensed snack bar on board.

If you wish, you can extend the rail journey by coach across the rugged Maniototo Plateau to Queenstown (6½ hours), from $138.

Another popular alternative is to take a mountain bike (no extra charge) and disembark at Middlemarch (only selected trains, but one-way fares available). From there you can negotiate the 150-km Otago Central Rail Trail (the former goldfields railway from Middlemarch to Clyde). It is a wonderful bike ride that includes over 60 bridges, viaducts and tunnels and much of Central Otago's classic scenery. The i-SITE visitor centre can supply all the relevant details.

Nurtured since 1914 and arguably the best in New Zealand, the 28-ha site is split into upper and lower gardens that straddle Signal Hill. Combined they form an interesting topography and all the usual suspects, with a particular bent on rhododendrons (at their best in October), plants from the Americas, Asia and Australia, native species, winter and wetland gardens. If you tire of the flora there is also a modern aviary complex, housing many exotic and native birds including the 'cheeky' kea and kaka parrots. Also on site are information points, a café and a small shop, all in the Lower Garden. Access to the Lower Garden is from Cumberland Street while the Upper Garden is reached via Lovelock Lane. The **Centennial Lookout** (6 km, 1½ hours' walk) and Lookout Point offer grand views of the harbour and the city, and are accessed via Signal Hill Road (beyond Lovelock Avenue).

While in the north of the city, you might like to visit the famed **Baldwin Street**, which at a gradient of nearly one in three, is reputed to be the steepest street in the world. It's worth a look, if only to work out the building methodology and what happens when the residents are eating at a table or in the bath. Head north via Great King Street then veer right at the Botanical Gardens on to North Road; Baldwin is about 1 km (10th street) on the right.

Orokunui Ecosanctuary

ⓘ *600 Blueskin Rd, Waitati (20 mins north of the city or via train, see Taieri Gorge Railway in box, above), T03-4821755, orokonui.org.nz. Daily 0930-1630, from $16, child $8, guided tours 1100 and 1330, from $30, child $15.*

The Orokonui Ecosanctuary was a project initiated in 2007 when 307 ha of protected habitat was encircled by 9 km of pest-proof fencing at a cost of $2.2 million. Once introduced mammals like rats, stoats and feral cats were eradicated and endangered native species were reintroduced. These species included birds like the Haast tokoeka kiwi, the kaka (a native parrot), the tom tit (piropiro) and rifleman (titpounamu). Many native fish and reptiles have also found sanctuary and thriving. There is a impressive visitor and information centre with interpretive displays as well as a small shop and café.

Otago Peninsula

The beautiful Otago Peninsula, which stretches 33 km northeast from Dunedin out into the Pacific Ocean, is as synonymous with wildlife as Dunedin is with Scotland. If there were any place that could honour the title of being the **wildlife** capital of the country, this would be it. It is home to an array of particularly rare species including the enchanting yellow-eyed penguin and the soporific Hooker's sea lion, as well the more common New Zealand fur seals. But without doubt the peninsula's star attraction is the breeding colony of royal albatross on **Taiaroa Head**, at the very tip of the peninsula. The first egg was laid here in 1920 and the now thriving colony (the only mainland breeding albatross colony in the world) offers an extraordinary opportunity to observe these supremely beautiful masters of flight and long-haul travel. An organized day trip to see some or all of these wildlife delights is highly recommended and will leave a precious and lasting memory. Besides wildlife, the principal attractions on the Otago Peninsula are historic **Larnach Castle** and the stunning vista of **Sandfly Bay**, as well as activities such as sea kayaking, cruising and walking.

For wildlife and general activity operator listings and maps consult the i-SITE Visitor Centre, page 77 and see What to do, page 85.

Royal Albatross Centre
ⓘ *Taiaroa Head, T03-478 0499, albatross.org.nz. Daily 0830-2100; seasonal; from $20, child $10. The observatory is closed 17 Sep-23 Nov each year, to allow the new season's birds to renew their pair bonds.*
Even before you enter the centre, if the conditions are right, you can see the great birds wheeling in from the ocean on wings that span over 3 m (the largest of any bird) and with a grace that defies the effort. The albatross centre has some superb exhibits that include static and audio-visual displays and even a live close-circuit TV feed from the occupied nests in the breeding season.

There are a number of tours available. The 1½-hour Unique Taiaroa tour includes an introductory video, a viewing of the colony from the hilltop observatory, and a look at the remains of Fort Taiaroa. This is a series of underground tunnels, fortifications and a 'disappearing gun' that were originally built in 1885 in response to a perceived threat of invasion from Tsarist Russia.

Yellow-eyed Penguin Conservation Reserve
ⓘ *Just before the Albatross Colony at Harington Point; for bookings contact the reserve direct, T03-478 0286, penguinplace.co.nz. Daily from 1015; May-Sep from 1515; $49, child $12.*
This is the most commercial operation, set on a private reserve with an expanding colony of about 200 birds, which has been carefully created and managed as a workable mix of tourism, commercialism and conservation. Once provided with an introductory talk you are then delivered by 4WD truck to the beach where an amazing network of covered tunnels and hides allows you to view the birds discreetly. The breeding season and adult moult periods (mid-Oct to late Feb and early May) are the best times to see large numbers, but you are almost guaranteed to see at least half a dozen birds all year round especially around dusk.

Otago Peninsula

N

1 km
1 mile

Where to stay
Larnach Lodge **1**

State Highway 1 North

George St

DUNEDIN

Octagon

Princes St

Portsmouth Dr

Andersons Bay Rd

Queens Dr

Monarch Wildlife Cruises & Tours

Doon St

Mussellburgh Rise

Ocean Gr

John Wilson Dr

Tomahawk Lagoon

Centre Rd

Karetai Rd

Seal Point

Portobello Rd

Highcliff Rd

Otago Harbour

Russell Bay

Glenfalloch

MacAndrew Bay

Mission Cove

Company Bay

Grassy Place

Broad Bay

Castlewood Rd

PUKEHIKI

Braidwo

Po Chal

Go Isla

Quarar Islan

La C

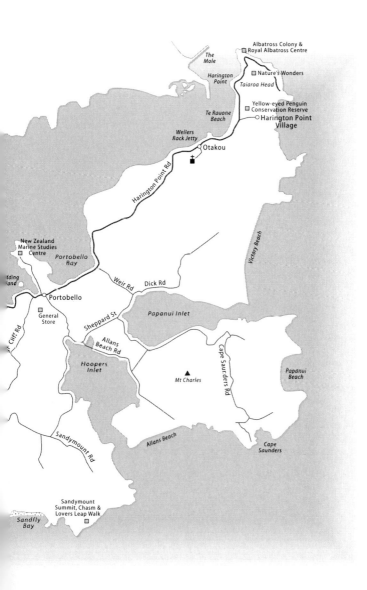

Albatross Colony &
Royal Albatross Centre

The Mole

Harington Point

Nature's Wonders

Taiaroa Head

Te Rauone Beach

Yellow-eyed Penguin
Conservation Reserve

Wellers Rock Jetty

Harington Point Village

Otakou

Harington Point Rd

New Zealand Marine Studies Centre

Portobello Bay

Weir Rd

Dick Rd

Victory Beach

Portobello

General Store

Sheppard St

Papanui Inlet

Papanui Beach

Allans Beach Rd

Hoopers Inlet

Mt Charles

Cape Saunders Rd

Allans Beach

Cape Saunders

Sandymount Rd

Sandymount Summit, Chasm & Lovers Leap Walk

Sandfly Bay

Dunedin and Otago Peninsua listings

For hotel and restaurant price codes and other relevant information, see pages 9-13.

Where to stay

Dunedin *p77, map p78*
$$$$ Corstorphine House, 23A Milburn St, Corstorphine, T03-487 1000, corstorphine.co.nz. An 1863 Edwardian luxury private hotel surrounded by 2.8 ha of private gardens and commanding great views across the city. The house is beautifully appointed throughout offering seven stylish themed suites from the Scottish or Egyptian to the art deco room and a restaurant.
$$$ Nisbet Cottage, 6A Eliffe Pl, Sheil Hill (east of the city centre), T03-4545169, natureguidesotago.co.nz. At the base of the Otago Peninsula, a short drive to the city centre. The congenial German hosts operate Otago Nature Guides (see What to do, page 85) and organize an attractive accommodation/nature tour package that includes the peninsula penguin colonies and albatross centre (2-night Nature Package from $645 per person). A choice of 2 tidy en suites sleeping 2-3, a guest lounge with open fire.

Motor parks
$$-$ Leith Valley Touring Park, 103 Malvern St (towards the northern end of town), T03-467 9936/0800-555331, leithvalleytouringpark.co.nz. An excellent little motor park in a sheltered setting next to the Leith Stream and about 2 km from the city centre. It has modern motel units, self-contained cabins, powered/tent sites, camp kitchen and a huge cosy guest lounge.

Otago Peninsula *p81, map p82*
$$$$-$$$ Larnach Lodge, 145 Camp Rd, T03-476 1616, larnachcastle.co.nz. Accommodation at Larnach Castle is some of the best in the region. The lodge offers beautifully appointed themed rooms from the Scottish Room with its tartan attire, to the Goldrush Room which comes complete with a king-size 'cart bed' made out of an original old cart found on the property. The views across the harbour and peninsula from every room are simply superb. Breakfast is served in the old stables; dinner is optional in the salubrious interior of the castle. Cheaper Stable Stay rooms with shared bathrooms in the former coach house are also available. Book well in advance.

Restaurants

Dunedin *p77, map p78*
$$$ Bell Pepper Blues, 474 Princes St, T03-474 0973. Lunch Wed-Fri, dinner Tue-Sat from 1830. Internationally recognized Chef Michael Coughlin has built up the reputation of this restaurant as one of Otago's best for almost 2 decades. Imaginative, mainly Pacific Rim cuisine.
$$$ Speights Brewery, 200 Rattray St, T03-477 7697, speights.co.nz. Combine a tour of the iconic Speights Brewery (Otago's most popular beer) with a meal in the brewery's own restaurant with the NZ classics like seafood chowder, blue cod, lamb shanks, steak, venison and vegetarian options.
$$ Scotia Restaurant and Whiskey Bar, Dunedin Railway Station, T03-477 770, scotiadunedin.co.nz. Mon-Fri 1100-late, Sat 1500-late. Fine Scottish-themed restaurant housed in the historic railway station. Scots classics like haggis and black pudding are of course on offer, yet there are other tastes to suit everyone, from venison, smoked beef, steak, salmon or salads and for sweet bread and butter pudding. After dinner sample 1 or 2 of the 300-odd whiskeys proudly showcased in the bar.

🎭 Entertainment

Dunedin *p77, map p78*
Cinema
Hoyts Cinema, 33 Octagon,
T03-477 7019, hoyts.co.nz.

⚙ What to do

Dunedin *p77, map p78*
Tour operators
Elm Wildlife Tours, Elm Lodge, T03-454
4121/0800-356563, elmwildlifetours.co.nz.
Provides a wide range of excellent award-
winning eco-tours of the peninsula and
the region. Its 5- to 6-hr peninsula tour is
fun and informative, yet non-commercial,
and gives you access to some of the most
scenic private land on the peninsula. From
$99 (albatross observatory and additional
activities extra). Pick-ups available.
Monarch Wildlife Cruises and Tours,
corner of Wharf and Fryatt streets, T03-
4774276, wildlife.co.nz. Award-winning
outfit offering a variety of trips from
1-7 hrs taking in all the main harbour
and peninsula sights.

Otago Peninsula *p81, map p82*
Tour operators
Otago Nature Guides, see the yellow-eyed
penguin colony at the beautiful Sandfly
Bay. Tours in conjunction with its fine B&B
accommodation in Nisbet Cottage (see
Where to stay, page 84).

🚍 Transport

Dunedin *p77, map p78*
Dunedin is 362 km south of Christchurch
and 217 km north of Invercargill via SH1.
Queenstown is 283 km south then west
via SH8.

ⓘ Directory

Dunedin *p77, map p78*
ATMs Represented along Princes and
George streets, with many accommodating
currency exchange services. **Travelex**,
346 George St, T03-4771532. **Hospital**
Dunedin Hospital, 201 Great King St,
T03-474 0999; **Doctor**, 95 Hanover St,
T03-479 2900 (pharmacy next door).

Northern and Central Otago

Northern and Central Otago are perhaps best described as 'in passing' destinations, worthy of a brief stop, but inevitably succumbing to the time-pressed angst to reach the main destinations of Dunedin or Queenstown.

The northern Otago town of Oamaru is often dubbed New Zealand's best-built town and offers a strange mix of grand colonial architecture and – believe it or not – wild penguins. A little further south the intrigue continues with the much-loved and wonderfully spherical Moeraki Boulders.

Central Otago is very often missed, and that alone is its appeal. The stark scenery of the Maniototo – which is the generic name for the flat high countryof the region – is very appealing, especially if some solitude is in order. In essence it can be the perfect antidote to the mayhem of Queenstown.

Oamaru

Oamaru is an unusual and appealing coastal town on the South Island's east coast, somehow befitting its position gracing the shores of Friendly Bay. Primarily functioning as a port and an agricultural service town, its modern-day tourist attractions lie in the strange combination of stone, architecture and penguins. Thanks to the prosperity of the 1860s-1890s, and the discovery of local limestone that could be easily carved and moulded, the early architects and stonemasons of Oamaru created a settlement rich in imposing, classic buildings, earning it the reputation of New Zealand's best-built town. Many old buildings remain, complete with Corinthian columns and gargantuan doorways, giving it a grand air. Add to that a small and congenial colony of yellow-eyed and blue penguins that waddle up to their burrows on the coast like dignified gents in 'tux and tails', and the town's appeal truly becomes apparent.

Most of the historic buildings and associated attractions are in the **Tyne-Harbour Street Historic Precinct** (begins at the southern end of Thames Street), which boasts the largest and best-preserved collection of historic commercial buildings in the country. There you will find a variety of tourist lures, from antique and craft outlets to second-hand bookstores, theatres and cafés.

But history aside, no visit to Oamaru would be complete without visiting its **penguin colonies**. The town has two very different species in residence – the enchanting little blue penguin (the smallest in the world) and the rare, larger, yellow-eyed penguin. There are two colonies and observation points, one at Bushy Beach (see below), where you can watch the yellow-eyed penguins from a hide for free, or the official harbourside **Oamaru Blue Penguin Colony** ① *T03-443 1195, penguins.co.nz, from 1000, self guided or guided, from $12, child $5, for dusk viewing penguins may arrive as late as 2100 in summer or as early as 1730 in winter,* that you must pay to access. There is a large covered stand from which you are given a brief talk before the penguins come ashore and waddle intently towards their burrows. The colony is accessed via Waterfront Road past the Historic Precinct.

The **Bushy Beach** yellow-eyed penguin colony and viewing hide is accessed on foot via the walkway at the end of Waterfront Road (30 minutes), or alternatively by car via Bushy Beach Road (end of Tyne Street from the Historic Precinct). The best time to view the birds is an hour or so before dawn and dusk when they come and go from their fishing expeditions.

For more information contact the **Oamaru i-SITE visitor centre** ① *corner of Itchen and Thames streets, T03-434 1656, tourismwaitaki.co.nz, Mon-Fri 0900-1800 (1700 Easter-Nov), Sat-Sun 1000-1700 (1600 Easter-Nov).* The centre has town maps and a wealth of information surrounding the historical buildings, local tours and things to see and do.

Moeraki and the boulders

On the coast about 40 km south of Oamaru are the **Moeraki Boulders**, a strange and much-photographed collection of spherical boulders that litter the beach. Although Maori legend has it that these boulders are tekaihinaki, or food baskets and sweet potatoes, science has determined that they are in fact 'septarian concretions', a rather classy name for 'rock gob-stoppers' left behind from the eroded coastal cliffs. To understand exactly how they are formed requires several PhDs in geology and physics, but you will find something near a layman's explanation at the **Moeraki Boulders Café Bar and Gift Shop** ① *T03-439 4827*, which is signposted just off SH1. The path to the boulders (200 m) starts at the car park and you are requested to provide a donation of $2.

The small fishing village of **Moeraki**, 3 km from the boulders, can be reached along the beach by foot (three hours return) or by car via SH1. Once a whaling settlement, first settled as long ago as 1836, it is a very pleasant little enclave and a great place to stay on the way south. For a great short walk head for the historic **lighthouse** (6 km) and its adjunct reserve for yellow-eyed penguins, which are best viewed at dusk or dawn. In the village itself **Fleur's Place** ⓘ *T03-439 4480, fleursplace.com*, by the pier is a wonderful lunch or dinner venue.

Dunedin to Alexandra via the 'Pigroot'

From Palmerston, 55 km north of Dunedin (via SH1 and the coast), SH85 turns inland to follow the 'Pigroot' (the old coach road between the coast and the goldfields) to Ranfurly and Alexandra, with a small diversion to St Bathans. A diversion from the conventional route south or west and a distance of 150 km from Palmerston to Alexandra it is seldom taken by tourists, which is exactly why you should consider it!

Like the MacKenzie Country to the north it has an aesthetic and a mood all of its own. Five mountain ranges encompass the region and within their embrace lies the expansive **Maniototo Plain** that became the mainstay of the region's economy once the 1860s gold boom was over.

Highlights along the way include the art deco buildings of **Ranfurly** (the largest town in the region), curling in **Naseby** (see page 89) and the historic buildings and **Blue Lake** in St Bathans.

Alexandra

At the junction of the Clutha and Manuherikia Rivers, Alexandra was one of the first gold mining towns to be established in Central Otago in 1862. Once the gold ran out at the end of the 1800s the orchardists moved in, making fruit growing Alexandra's modern-day industry. The town is at its best in autumn when the riverside willows and poplars, bathe the valley in another golden hue. Alexandra serves as the principal gateway to the **Otago Central Rail Trail**, which is becoming an increasingly popular multi-day mountain-biking adventure.

The main attraction in town is the **Central Stories Museum and Art Gallery** housed in the same building as the **i-SITE visitors centre** ⓘ *21 Centennial Av, Pioneer Park, Alexandra, T03-448 6230, centralstories.com*.

Clyde

Just 10 km west of Alexandra is the pretty and historic village of Clyde. Backed by the concrete edifice of the Clyde Dam, which incarcerates **Lake Dunstan**. It offers a pleasant stop on the way to Queenstown or Wanaka. Originally called Dunstan and the hub of the rich Dunstan Goldfields, it assumed its present name in the late 1860s. Clyde in Scottish Gaelic is Clutha, which is the river that once flowed freely through the Cromwell Gorge and is the longest in the South Island. Amidst Clyde's very pleasant aesthetics are a number of historic old buildings including the Town Hall (1868), various pioneer cottages and a handful of its once 70 hotels. The Old Courthouse on Blyth Street is another fine example that was built in 1864.

Cromwell

At the head of Lake Dunstan, 23 km to the north of Clyde, is the tidy – and fruity – little town of Cromwell. Cromwell is faced with five very large dilemmas. The first four are a pear, an apple, a nectarine and a delightfully pert pink bottom (which we can only presume is an apricot) and the fifth is the town's proximity to Queenstown. It is the latter of course with which it struggles the most. Just how do you stop any tourist so intent on reaching perhaps the busiest tourist town in the country? Well, it seems some bright spark (there is always one) thought a sculpture of four man-eating pieces of fruit and celebrating the regions fruit-growing prowess (or indeed just a large and lovely pink bum) might be a great idea? Does it work? You decide.

Anyway, behemoth fruit aside, the former gold town, Cromwell, was originally called 'The Junction' due to its position at the confluence of the **Clutha** and **Kawarau rivers**. These important bodies of water form an integral part of the South Island's hydropower scheme. The museum attached to the i-SITE visitors' centre focuses on the early history and building of the Clyde Dam and is worth a look. The decision to build the dam in the 1980s, using Cromwell as the accommodation base, brought many changes to the town and gave rise to a mix of old-world charm and modern, tidy aesthetics. The main attraction in the town itself is the **Old Cromwell Town Precinct** at the end of Melmore Terrace and at the point where the two rivers merge. Several former buildings have been restored and now house local cafés and craft shops 1000-1630, free.

The **Goldfields Mining Centre** ① *SH6 west, 6 km towards Queenstown T03-4451038, goldfieldsmining.co.nz, daily 0900-1700, self-guided and guided tours from $20, child $7.50*, provides the opportunity to see historic gold workings, a Chinese settlers' village, gold stamper batteries and a sluice gun. You can also pan for gold, go horse trekking or jet boating.

As well as its many orchards, the immediate area is also home to a number of **vineyards**, particularly around the pretty village of **Bannockburn** just to the south of Cromwell. It's a fine spot for lunch and the i-SITE visitor centre has full listings.

Northern and Central Otago listings

For hotel and restaurant price codes and other relevant information, see pages 9-13.

⏰ What to do

Dunedin to Alexandra via the 'Pigroot' *p88*
Curling
The ancient Scottish game of curling has been a central feature of the Maniototo since the late 1870s, the first reported game was 6 Jul 1878.
Maniototo Curling International, 1057 Channel Rd, Naseby, T03-444 9878, curling. co.nz. A state-of-the-art indoor curling rink

that now serves as the hub for the ancient sport in New Zealand. It is great fun even for beginners and you can give it a go from $20 per hr.

Alexandra *p88*
Cycling
Otago Central Rail Trail, otagocentral railtrail.co.nz. Various transport operators provide luggage and bike pick-up or drop-offs and bike hire (and/or guided tours) for both trails including: **Altitude Adventures**, T03-448 8917, altitude adventures.co.nz and **Trail Journeys**, T03-449 2150/0800-724587, trail journeys.co.nz.

Queenstown and around

Ladies and gentlemen, fasten your seat belts and welcome to Queenstown – Adrenalin Central, Thrillsville, New Zealand – the adventure capital of the world. You are perhaps studying this guide in your hotel or motor home with a pained expression trying to decide which of the 150-odd activities to try and, more importantly, how your wallet can possibly cope? But first things first: look out of the window. Where else in the world do you have such accessible scenery? And all that is free.

Queenstown has come a long way since gold secured its destiny in the 1860s. It is now the biggest tourist draw in New Zealand and considered one of the top (and almost certainly the most scenic) adventure venues in the world. Amidst the stunning setting of mountain and lake, over one million visitors a year partake in a staggering range of activities from a sedate steamboat cruise to the heart-stopping bungee jump. You can do almost anything here, from a gentle round of golf to paddling down a river in what looks like a blow-up carrot. Add to that a superb range of accommodation, services, restaurants and cafés.

Arriving in Queenstown

Getting there

Queenstown airport ⓘ *T03-4423505, queenstown airport.co.nz*, is 8 km east of the town in Frankton. It receives direct daily flights from Auckland, Christchurch, Wellington and Dunedin. From the airport, **ConnectaBus** ⓘ *T03-4414471*, costs $6 into town. **Kiwi Shuttle** ⓘ *T03-4422107*, serves the airport door to door. A **taxi** ⓘ *T03-4427788*, will set you back about $40. **Regional buses** arrive and depart from The Station, corner of Camp and Shotover Streets.

Tourist information

Queenstown Travel and i-SITE visitor centre ⓘ *below the Clock Tower, corner of Shotover and Camp streets, T0800-668 888, T03-442 4100, queenstown-vacation.com and queenstown-nz.co.nz, open 0700-1900 (winter 1800)*. DoC ⓘ *37 Shotover St, T03-4427935, doc.govt.nz*, is next to the **Information and Track Centre** ⓘ *37 Shotover St, T03-442 9708, infotrack. co.nz, daily 0830-1900, winter Mon-Fri 0900-1700, Sat-Sun 0930-1630*, which provides up-to-date information on local walks and major tramps, and deals with transportation and hut bookings. It also offers gear hire and has the latest weather forecasts. For activity listings, see page 98.

Places in Queenstown → See map, page 92.

Perhaps the best place to start is the **Skyline Gondola** ⓘ *Brecon St, T03-4410101, skyline. co.nz, 0900-dusk, gondola $25, child $14*, that delivers you to the Skyline Complex 450 m above the town on Bob's Peak. It boasts a world-class view and has a host of activities including The Ledge Bungy, The Luge, The Sky-Swing, paragliding and helicopter flight-seeing. The Kiwi Haka Maori performance is also based at Skyline with 30-minute shows nightly for $59 (includes gondola) and the option of an all-inclusive dinner (including show and gondola) for $110. Other on-site amenities include shops, a café (0930-2100) and a restaurant (see page 97). A good time to go up is just before sunset when the golden rays slowly creep up the **Remarkables range** and the town's lights come on.

Back down to earth and at the base of the gondola you might like to see the obligatory kiwi and friends in the **Kiwi Birdlife Park** ⓘ *Brecon St, T03-4428059, kiwibird.co.nz, daily summer 0900- 1800, winter 0900-1730, $38, child $19*. Set in 8 ha of pine forest it displays all the usual suspects, including kiwi, owls, parakeets, tui and kea.

The waterfront is always a great buzz of activity. It hosts several lake-based activities including jet boating and fishing but the major draw is the iconic and delightful **TSS Earnslaw** ⓘ *tssearnslaw.co.nz*, (TSS stands for Two Screw Steamer). Named after the highest peak in the region, Mount Earnslaw (2819 m), she was launched at the most southerly end of **Lake Wakatipu**, Kingston, in 1912 and burns 1 ton of coal per hour. Despite her propensity to belch half of New Zealand's 'Kyoto-nasty smoke quota' into the air she is a lovely sight indeed and there are a number of cruising options available (see page 99).

Opposite the Steamer Wharf the **Queenstown Gardens** are well worth a visit and offer some respite from the crowds. There are oaks, some stunning sequoias and 1500 roses planted in 26 named rose beds.

Around Queenstown

To the north, at the head of Lake Wakatipu, the small and far less developed settlement of **Glenorchy** (47 km) is the gateway to some of the country's most impressive scenery and several of its best tramping tracks, including the Routeburn, the Greenstone, Caples and Rees-Dart. But without even needing to don boots and gaiters you can explore the immediate area or partake in several activities including jet-boat trips, canoeing or horse

Queenstown

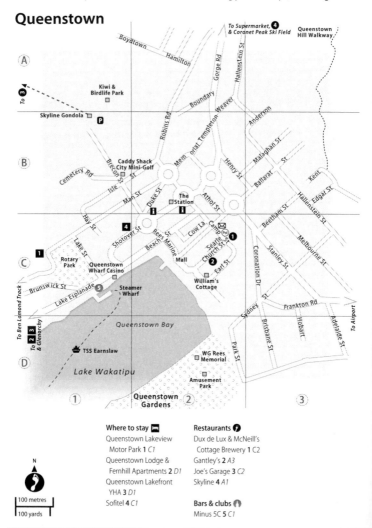

Where to stay 🛏	Restaurants 🍴
Queenstown Lakeview Motor Park **1** *C1*	Dux de Lux & McNeill's Cottage Brewery **1** *C2*
Queenstown Lodge & Fernhill Apartments **2** *D1*	Gantley's **2** *A3*
Queenstown Lakefront YHA **3** *D1*	Joe's Garage **3** *C2*
Sofitel **4** *C1*	Skyline **4** *A1*
	Bars & clubs 🍸
	Minus 5C **5** *C1*

Queenstown for free

The following are some great activities in and around Queenstown that won't cost more than a coffee and a few litres of petrol.

Even if the closest you want to come to bungee jumping is the elastic in your own underwear then you can still derive terrific entertainment from simply spectating. The best place to do that is at the original bungee site 23 km south of the town at the Kawarau Suspension Bridge run by the ubiquitous AJ Hackett Bungy Company. The multi-million dollar centre is testament to the commercial success of the concept in the last 20 years.

Feeling fit? You can walk (one hour one way) up to the Skyline Complex via the Ben Lomond Track, which starts on Lomond Crescent (via Brunswick Street off the Lake Esplanade). The summit (1748 m) ascent is a seven-hour return hike.

Take a drive to the Coronet Peak ski-field (18 km). The views are spectacular and you can watch the hangliders launch themselves in to the air. The short diversion to look down the barrel of the Shotover Valley (Skippers Road) is also worth it, but unless you have a 4WD vehicle don't go any further. On the way back, just beyond the Shotover Bridge, take a right and follow the road to the rivers edge. From there walk upstream to the waterfall and gorge lookout. The Shotover Jet comes up to the falls and they are also the last feature on many of the rafting runs. Don't stand too close to the river's edge – the jet boat drivers just love soaking unsuspecting spectators, especially with expensive camera gear.

trekking (see pages 98-101). The Dart River Basin reached almost legendary status when it was used as a set for the *Lord of the Rings* trilogy, but you don't need to know your Orcs from your Nazguls to appreciate its innate natural beauty, nor muse upon the small settlement of **Paradise** to agree that it was indeed aptly named.

Of a more historic bent is the small former gold rush settlement of **Arrowtown**, which sits tucked away in the corner of the Wakatipu Basin, 23 km south of Queenstown. It has a fascinating history that is now well presented in the village museum and complemented nicely with a main street that looks almost like a Hollywood film set. The origins of Arrowtown go back to 1862 when prospector William Fox made the first rich strike in the Arrow River Valley – a find that soon brought over 7000 other hopefuls to the area. The first few weeks of mining produced 90 kg alone. But history and aesthetics aside, behind the old doors and down the alley ways you will find a surprising number of fine shops, cafés, restaurants and pubs in which you can let the infectious and exhausting mania of Queenstown quietly subside.

Wanaka

Wanaka is almost unfeasibly pleasant and has to rank as one of the most desirable places in New Zealand. With the lake of the same name lapping rhythmically at its heels and its picture-postcard mountain backdrops – bordering as it does the Mount Aspiring National Park – it is easy to understand why Wanaka is such a superb place to visit, or indeed live. In recent years Wanaka has seen a boom in both real estate sales and tourism, but it is reassuring that its manic neighbour, Queenstown, will always keep growth in check. But for a while at least, Wanaka is just perfect: not too busy, not too quiet; developed but not spoilt, and a place for all to enjoy. Although now you would never guess it, Wanaka's history goes back to the 1860s when it played an important role as a service centre for the region's itinerant gold miners. Today, its principal resources are activities and its miners are tourists. Year-round, there is a multitude of things to do from watersports and tramping in summer to skiing in winter. But it can also be the perfect place to relax and recharge your batteries beside the lake.

Wanaka town centre borders the very pretty **Lake Wanaka**. The aesthetics are awesome and the waters are also a prime attraction for boaties, water-skiers, kayakers and windsurfers. On the way into town you cannot fail to miss New Zealand's 'Leaning Tower of Wanaka', the centerpiece of **Stuart Landsborough's Puzzling World** ① *T03-443 7489, puzzlingworld. com, 0830-1730, $15, child $10, shop and café*. This is a madcap and puzzling conglomerate of mazes, illusions and holograms that is worth a muse. The toilets and 'Hall of Following Faces' are particularly engaging.

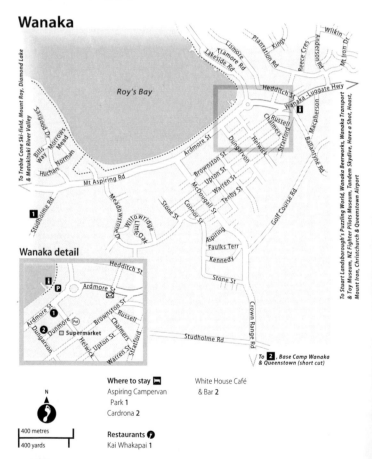

Wanaka

Where to stay 🛏
Aspiring Campervan Park **1**
Cardrona **2**

White House Café & Bar **2**

Restaurants 🍴
Kai Whakapai **1**

The Rob Roy glacier walk

If you haven't time or the energy for any of the major tramps, there is one day-walk in the Mount Aspiring National Park that is accessible from Wanaka and quite simply a 'must do'. From Wanaka drive (or arrange transportation) to the Raspberry Creek Car Park in the West Matukituki Valley (one hour). From there follow the river, west to the footbridge over the river and up in to the Rob Roy Valley. From here the track gradually climbs, following the chaotic Rob Roy River, through beautiful rainforest, revealing the odd view of the glacier above. After about 1½ hours you will reach the tree line and enter a superb hidden valley rimmed with solid rock walls of waterfall and ice. It is simply stunning and well deserving of the label 'The Jewel of the Park'. Keep your eyes, your ears open for kea, though they may find you before you find them. After some thorough investigation of the area, you can then retrace your steps back down the valley to the Matukituki River and the car park (five hours return). Alpine Coachlines (alpinecoachlines. co.nz) can shuttle you to Raspberry Creek for a rather pricey $70 return, T03-443 7966, alpinecoachlines.co.nz. Departs 0845 and 1300 returning 1000 and 1445.

Some 8 km east on SH6, surrounding Wanaka airfield, are a couple of interesting museums. The **New Zealand Fighter Pilots Museum** ① *T03-4437010, nzfpm.co.nz, daily 0900-1600, $20, child $5*, honours the lives (and deaths) of New Zealand fighter pilots and provides an insight into general aviation history. Around the museum you might like to sit and watch terrified faces turn to ecstatic ones at the base of Skydive Wanaka (see page 100).

Wanaka i-SITE visitor centre ① *in the Log Cabin on the lakefront, 100 Ardmore St, T03-443 1233, lakewanaka.co.nz, daily 0830-1830, winter 0930-1630.*

Mount Aspiring National Park

Like most of New Zealand's majestic national parks, Mount Aspiring has an impressive list of vital statistics. First designated in 1964 the park has been extended to now cover 3500 sq km, making it New Zealand's third largest. It contains five peaks over 2600 m, including Aspiring itself – at 3027 m, the highest outside the Mount Cook range. It contains over 100 glaciers and enjoys an annual rainfall of between 1-6 m a year. It is home to some unique wildlife like the New Zealand falcon, the kea and the giant weta. It is part of a World Heritage Area of international significance – the list just goes on. But, it is not figures that best describe this park. It is without doubt the names, words and phrases associated with it. How about Mount Awful, Mount Dreadful, or Mount Dispute? Mount Chaos perhaps? Then there is the Valley of Darkness, Solitude Creek and the Siberia River. How about the Pope's Nose or the mind boggling Power Knob? This is a wilderness worthy of investigation and well beyond mere imagination; a park of stunning and remote beauty. Enough said. Get in there and enjoy, but go prepared.

The **DoC Mount Aspiring National Park visitor centre** ① *Upper Ardmore St at the junction with McPherson St, T03-443 7660, doc.govt.nz, daily 0830-1630*, deals with all national park/tramping hut bookings and local walks information. An up-to-date weather forecast is also available.

Queenstown and around listings

For hotel and restaurant price codes and other relevant information, see pages 9-13.

○ Where to stay

Queenstown *p91, map p92*

Despite a healthy range of accommodation and around 9000 beds in Queenstown, it is essential to book 2 or 3 days in advance in mid-summer or during the height of the ski season (especially during the Winter Festival in mid-Jul).

$$$$-$$$ Sofitel, 8 Duke St, T03-450 0045, sofitelqueenstown.com. One of the most celebrated hotels sitting in prime position just above the town centre. Luxury rooms, suites and penthouses furnished in European style and in warm shades of beige and brown marry well with the views. The class extends to the facilities and the in-house restaurant, but perhaps, just perhaps, your abiding memory will be of its famous 'little' boy's room in the lobby (go on girls – have a peek!).

$$$-$$ Queenstown Lodge and Fernhill Apartments, Sainsbury Rd (a little further out at the west end of town), Fernhill, T03-442 7107/T0800-756343, queenstownlodge.co.nz. Reasonably priced ski lodge-style property located at the western fringe of town. It is quiet, has off-street parking, a pizza restaurant, spa, sauna and most of the rooms offer excellent views across Lake Wakatipu. The lodge also administers a self-contained apartment complex offering good value 1- to 3-bedroom options and clients then have full use of lodge facilities.

$$ Kinloch Lodge, T03-442 4900, kinlochlodge.co.nz. Historic lakeside budget lodge and the perfect base from which to explore the area before (and especially after) tramping the Routeburn or Greenstone tracks. Tidy doubles (the heritage doubles are very small), twins and shared dorms, all the usual facilities as well as a outdoor hot tub, a café/restaurant and

a small shop. Road or water taxi transport is available from Glenorchy and local activities arranged. Really well managed and a memorable stay is just about guaranteed.

$$ Queenstown Lakefront YHA, 80 Lake Esplanade (at the western end of town), T03-4428413, yha.co.nz. Deservedly popular and the larger of 2 YHAs in town. Alpine lodge style with a wide range of comfortable shared, twin and double rooms and modern facilities in a quiet location overlooking Lake Wakatipu. Limited off-street parking.

Motor parks

$$$-$ Queenstown Lakeview Motor Park, off Brecon St, T03-4427252, T0800-482735, holidaypark.net.nz. After a revamp this park has increased in popularity and stature. The complex is the closest park to the town centre (2 mins) and includes tidy and good-value studio units, en suite cabins, luxury flats, as well as the standard powered/tent sites. There is a spacious kitchen block with internet and lockable food cupboards.

Wanaka *p93, map p94*

$$$ Cardrona Hotel, Crown Range (Cardrona) Rd, 26 km from Wanaka, T03-443 8153, cardronahotel.co.nz. A little way out but well worth the journey, especially in winter when fires are lit in the gardens from dusk to welcome those coming off the ski field. The 16 comfortable en suite double rooms in the old stables are charming and front a beautiful enclosed garden and courtyard. There is a great rustic restaurant and bar attached and a spa. Bookings are essential.

Motor parks

$$ Aspiring Campervan Park, Studholme Rd, T03-443 7766, campervanpark.co.nz. An entirely different and new concept in motor camps. A Qualmark 5-star, it charges well beyond the standard for a powered site, but has all mod cons including a spa (included in tariff) that looks out towards the mountains. Modern lodge, motel and tourist flats are also available.

🍴 Restaurants

Queenstown *p91, map p92*
$$$ Gantley's, Arthur's Point Rd, T03-442 8999, gantleys.co.nz. Daily from 1830. A very romantic affair set in a historic stone building 7 km out of town towards Arrowtown. Award winning, and its wine list, like its cuisine, is superb.
$$$ Skyline Restaurant, Skyline Gondola Complex, Brecon St, T03-441 0101, skyline. co.nz. Daily lunch buffet 1200-1400, dinner from 1800. Offers a 6-course 'Taste of New Zealand' buffet, which includes roast meats, seafood, local produce and salads followed by dessert and cheeseboard. The views are exceptional, even at night.
$$$-$$ Dux de Lux & McNeill's Cottage Brewery, 14 Church St, T03-4429688, thedux.co.nz/queenstown. Daily from 1130. A nice mix of heritage and atmosphere, it's another award-winner with a good selection of gourmet pizzas, open fire outside, live bands at the weekend and, of course, some fine home-brewed ales.
$$ Joe's Garage, Searle Lane, T03-442 5282, joes.co.nz. The secret hang out for locals and noted for its great coffee and light meals.

🍸 Bars and clubs

Queenstown *p91, map p92*
$$ Minus 5C, Steamer Wharf, T03-442 6050. Daily from 1030. Sit back with a cocktail in this beautifully sculpted ice cavern. Entry costs $30 includes the first drink and you are of course kitted out with warm jackets and gloves. Naturally this is more a tourist attraction than a conventional bar; so don't expect to settle in for a session or a game of darts.

Wanaka *p93, map p94*
$$$ White House Café and Bar, corner of Dunmore and Dungarvon streets, T03-443 9595. Daily from 1100. Deservedly popular with an imaginative Mediterranean/Middle Eastern menu with vegetarian options. Fine wine list.
$$ Kai Whakapai, corner Helwick and Ardmore streets, T03-443 7795. Good blackboard fare, coffee and a great spot to watch the world go by.

🎭 Entertainment

Queenstown *p91, map p92*
Cinema
Embassy Cinema, 11 The Mall, T03-442 9994.

Wanaka *p93, map p94*
Cinema
Paradiso Cinema and Café, 1 Ardmore St, T03-443 1505, paradiso.net.nz. Famous for its one-of-a-kind movie offerings, complete with comfy chairs and homemade ice cream. The café is as laid back.

🎉 Festivals

Queenstown *p91, map p92*
Jul Queenstown Winter Festival winter festival.co.nz. Queenstown's most famous and popular event (9 days), which of course has its focus on skiing, but also involves many other forms of entertainment.

Wanaka *p93, map p94*
Mar Warbirds Over Wanaka, T03-4438619, warbirdsoverwanaka.com. New Zealand's premier air show is held biannually (next in 2014). The venue is the airfield, which hosts a wide variety of visiting 'birds', but also blows the dust off the New Zealand Fighter Pilots Museum's very own Spitfire.

◎ Shopping

Glenorchy *p92*
Made in Glenorchy Fur Products,
corner Mull and Argyle St, T03-442
7772, glenorchy-fur.co.nz. Have you
been wanting to get your dear mother
or girlfriend that special homecoming
present? Well, if so you have found 'ideal
presents utopia'. Amid the obvious (and
lovely) scarves, rugs and gloves are a fine
range of possum fur nipple warmers.
They are the genuine article and come
in a marvellous array of colours.

◎ What to do

Queenstown and around *p90*
So, where do you start?
Well, there are over 150 activities to choose
from, with everything from the tipples of a
wine tour to the ripples of jet boating. And
Queenstown is not just geared up for the
young and the mad. There are activities to
suit all ages, from infant to octogenarian
and from the able to the less able. If a
91-year-old can do a bungee jump, surely
the possibilities are endless? Of course
it is the bungee that made Queenstown
famous. If you are prepared to make 'the
jump' and have been saving your pennies
to do so, then it is here that you must finally
pluck up the courage. Heights vary from
40 m to 134 m, and if there is any advice to
give (other than psychological and financial
counselling) it is: do it in style and 'go high'.

The big 4 activities in Queenstown are
considered to be the bungee, jet boating,
rafting and flight-seeing. However, don't
only consider what you are 'supposed' to
do, but also what most others don't do –
and also what you can do for free (see box,
page 93).

The best advice is to head to the unbiased
Queenstown Travel and Visitor Centre (see
page 91), have a chat and avail yourself
of the leaflets and information, then retire
quietly to a coffee shop for a small nervous

breakdown. Above all don't ruin it by
rushing or being impulsive. Think before you
jump! Oh, and one other thing, there are no
refunds if you do end up holding on the bus
driver like a koala does a tree.

The following provide an outline of the
main activities and a sample of operators
to wet the appetite. It is by no means
comprehensive. Also note combo packages
are available and are often good value.

Ballooning
Sunrise Balloons, T03-4420781,
ballooningnz.com. Offer the standard
and sedate 3-hr flight with champagne
breakfast for $445, child $295.

Bungee jumping
A J Hackett, 'The Station', corner of
Shotover and Camp streets, T03-4424007/
T0800-286495, ajhackett.com. A J Hackett
and associates in 1988 created the 1st
commercial bungee jump in the world
at Kawarau Bridge about 12 km east
of Queenstown. Although perhaps the
most famous spot and certainly the most
accessible, at 43 m it is now dwarfed by
most of the others. Since 1988 Hackett has
created several other sites in and around
Queenstown from the Ledge at the Skyline
Gondola Complex to the highest (ground
based) 134-m Nevis Highwire. Jump prices
range from $180 to a cool $260 for the Nevis.
Given the prices the best advice is to 'go
high'– at the Nevis – it is simply rude not to.

It hasn't taken long for the Great
Adrenalin Professors to realize that
wetting your pants at high speed need not
necessarily occur at vertical angles alone,
so the fiendishly clever-and-rich chappies
have now come up with various swing
contraptions. The 2 options are:
Nevis Arc, A J Hackett, above.
Shotover Canyon Swing, Shotover Canyon
Swing, T03-442 6990, T0800-279464,
canyonswing.co.nz. We won't get in to the
technical details, suffice to say that the
swing is 109 m high, with a 60-m freefall,

200-m arc using various jump styles from the Backwards and the Forwards, to the Downright Insane... Prices start at around $199, spectators $20.

Cruising

It won't take you long to spot the delightful *TSS Earnslaw* plying the waters of Lake Wakatipu from the Steamer Wharf in Queenstown Bay. A standard 1½-hr cruise heads west across the lake to its southern edge to the Walter Peak Station. It departs from the Steamer Wharf, Oct-Apr every 2 hrs from 1000-2000 (reduced winter schedule), from $55, child $22. A 3½-hr cruise, plus a farm tour of the Walter Peak Station which is designed to give an insight into typical Kiwi farming life (and to access lots of affectionate animals), costs $75, child $22. With a BBQ it's $20 extra. A 4-hr evening dinner cruise costs $115, child $57.50. There are also 40-min horse trekking and wagon rides available at Walter Peak from $110 (all inclusive). **Real Journeys**, Steamer Wharf, T0800-656503, realjourneys.co.nz.

Flight-seeing and aerobatics

There are numerous options available either by helicopter or fixed wing and you are advised to shop around. If you don't have time to reach Milford Sound by road then a scenic flight is highly recommended. Note that there are numerous fly-cruise-fly and bus-cruise-fly options on offer to Milford (ask at the i-SITE). Other flight-seeing options include Mt Cook and the glaciers, Mt Aspiring National Park and Lord of the Rings filming locations. Prices range from a 30-min local flight costing from about $200 to the full 4-hr Milford Sound and Mt Cook experience, from about $400; shop around.

Fixed-wing operators offering flights to Milford Sound include: **Air Fiordland**, T03-4423404, airfiordland.com and **Air Milford**, T03-4422351, airmilford .co.nz. A *Lord of the Rings* Trilogy Trail is offered by the personable owners and staff of **Glenorchy Air**, Queenstown Airport, T03-442 2207, glenorchy.net.nz, trilogytrail.com, from $148, child $74.

Helicopter operators include: **Glacier Southern Lakes** T03-442 3016/ T0800-801616, heli-flights.co.nz; **The Helicopter Line**, T03-442 3034, T0800-500575 helicopter.co.nz and **Over The Top Helicopters**, T0800-123359, T03-4422233, flynz.co.nz. The latter also offer heli-fishing and heli-skiing options.
Vintage Tigermoth Flights, based at the airfield, T03-4434043, T0508-4359464, classicflights.co.nz. Offers something a little bit different, from $235.

Horse trekking

The best location for scenery is Glenorchy. **Dart Stables**, based in Glenorchy, T03-442 5688, dartstables.com, offer several attractive options including 2-hr trek ($129), 1½-hr 'Ride of the Rings' ($169).

Jet boating

Jet boating is one of the 'Big 4' activities in Queenstown and, other than the thrills of the precipitous Shotover Gorge, there are also other independent operations on the Kawarau from Queenstown itself and the superb aesthetics of the Dart River. For thrills the Shotover is recommended; for scenery the Dart River.
Shotover Jet, The Station, Shotover St, T03-442 8570, T0800-SHOTOVER, shotoverjet.com (from $129); Kawarau Jet Marine Pde (lakeside), T03-442 6142, T0800-529272, kjet.co.nz, from $110; and Dart River Safaris, Glenorchy T03-442 9992 / T0800-327853, dartriver.co.nz, 3-6 hrs from $219, child $119 (includes transport from Queenstown).

Kingston Flyer

The famous vintage steam train puffs along for 1¼ hrs on a 14-km track from Kingston, 47 km south of Queenstown from Sep to mid-May, daily 1000 and 1330, morning pick-ups available from Queenstown.

Return ride $60, child $30, one-way $40/$20.
T03-248 8848, kingstonflyer.co.nz.

Mountain biking
There are many options, from the manic
heli-bike to the low-level mundane.
Independent hire and self-guided trail
maps are also available. Operators include:
Fat Tyre Adventures, T0800-328897, fat-
tyre.co.nz and **Vertigo Mountain Biking**, 4
Brecon St, T03-442 8378, gravityaction.com.

Mountaineering and rock climbing
Mount Aspiring Guides, T03-443 9422,
aspiringguides.com. Offers a range of trips
and packages all year round. Mt Aspiring
$3650 2:1 client-guide ratio, with flights.
Wanaka Rock, T03-443 6411, wanakarock.
co.nz. Courses include introductory (½ day
$140), and abseil (half-day $140).

Rafting
There is a glut of rafting operators, all trying
to lure you with their ineluctable inflatables
with most plying the rapids of the Shotover,
Kawarau and Landsborough with such
enchanting highlights as The Toilet and
The Sharks Fin. A half-day adventure will
cost around $185. Shop around for the best
deal. **Challenge Rafting**, T03-442 7318/
T0800-423836, raft.co.nz; **Extreme Green
Rafting**, T03-442 8517, extremegreenrafting.
co.nz and **Queenstown Rafting**, T03-442
9792, rafting.co.nz.

River sledging and surfing
River surfing is the cunningly simple
concept of replacing a raft with your own
personal body board. It is great fun and
provides a far more intimate experience
with the water. River sledging involves
more drifting as opposed to surfing and
provides more buoyancy. Costs from $150.
Companies include:
Frogz Have More Fun, T03-4412318/
0800-437649, frogz.co.nz.
Mad Dog, T03-4427797,
river boarding.co.nz.

Serious Fun, T03-442 5262/
0800-737468 , riversurfing.co.nz.

Skiing
Wanaka has several great ski fields within
50 km of the town and encompassing
standard ski and board slopes, cross-
country and even a specialist snowboard
freestyle park at the new Snow Park.
Cardrona, Snow Park and Snow Farm are
to the south, while Treble Cone is to the
northwest. For general information and
snow reports check out snow.co.nz; nzski.
com; snow parknz.com; snowfarmnz.com
or skilakewanaka.com.

Skydiving
Tandem Skydive Wanaka, T03-443 7207,
T0800-786877, skydivenz.com. One of the
best operators in the country and operates
out of the airfield from heights of 12,000 ft
($299) and 15,000 ft ($399).

Tours
New Zealand Nomad Safaris, T03-442
6699, T0800-688222 nomad safaris.co.nz.
Offers an excellent range of 4WD tours
taking in some of the stunning scenery
used in *The Lord of the Rings* film trilogy.
Other tours concentrate on gold-mining
remnants along the 'entertaining' Skippers
Canyon Rd and quad bike tours.
Queenstown Wine Trail Company, T03-
442 3799, queenstownwinetrail.co.nz.
Visits all the main Kawarau Valley vineyards,
3-5 hrs from $129.

Tramping
Queenstown is a principal departure point
for the Routeburn Greenstone-Caples and
Rees-Dart Tracks. For detailed information,
hut and transportation bookings visit
the **Information and Track Centre**
(see page 91). **Guided Walks New
Zealand**, T03-4427126, nzwalks.com
and **Ultimate Hikes**, The Station,
T0800-659255, ultimate hikes.co.nz.

Wellbeing

If you can simply take no more action, try a soothing massage or a beauty treatment with **Body Sanctum**, 12 Man St, T03-442 8006, bodysanctum.co.nz, or **Hush Spa**, Level 2, corner of Gorge and Robins roads, T03-409 0901, hushspa.co.nz. Massage treatments start at 30 mins from $70. Also worth considering are the **Onsen Hot Pools**, 9351/160 Arthurs Point Rd; **Arthurs Point**, T03-442 5707, onsen.co.nz.

⊖ Transport

Queenstown *p91, map p92*
By road, Queenstown is 486 km from Christchurch, 283 km from Dunedin, 68 km from Wanaka and 170 km from Te Anau (Milford Sound 291 km).

See also Arriving in Queenstown, page 91.

① Directory

Queenstown *p91, map p92*
ATMs Represented along Camp St.
Hospital Douglas St, Frankton, T03-442 3053; **Queenstown Medical Centre**, 9 Isle St, Queenstown, T03-441 0500.

Southland

Fiordland, New Zealand's largest national park, has a moody magnificence, with its high mountains, forested hills and deep inlets such as Doubtful Sound and Milford Sound. The latter is the most accessible of the park's 14 fiords and one of the country's biggest visitor attractions. Further east, in contrast, is one of New Zealand's most prosperous dairy regions, which is also famous for its fishing.

Te Anau

Te Anau sits on the shores of New Zealand's second largest lake (of the same name) and at the edge of the magnificent wilderness of the Fiordland National Park. Serving as the parks pretty little gatekeeper – and in particular the legendary State Highway 94 (SH94) to Milford Sound – poor Te Anau suffers a bit from seasonal 'affected' disorder. In summer it's utterly manic and it's not hard to understand why. With up to 70 coaches a day passing through en route to Milford Sound that's one mighty big toilet stop. But that's not all. Added to that are the plentiful perambulations of the species **Copious beardicus** – or 'trampers'. You see Te Anau is also considered by many as the walking (or tramping) capital of the world. Within a 100-km radius you have access to literally thousands of kilometres of world-class tramping tracks with such legendary names as The Kepler, Routeburn and the Milford (itself once declared by National Geographic as the best multi-day walk in the world).

But then, come autumn, for little Te Anau the proverbial golden leaf falls from the tourism tree. With the absence of a ski field to woo winter visitors the town is like an unused holiday house, with only its caretaker, waiting and wanting to turn the heating on again. It can be quite depressing and try getting a pint of milk at ten at night!

It can initially seem a rather dull little town, but once you acquaint yourself with its tidy centre, spacious open areas and beautiful lake views (and yes, its spiffy new supermarket) your desire to move on quite so hastily will fade.

Te Anau

To 🛈, Te Anau Downs (27 km) & Milford Sound (120 km)

Matai St
McKerrow St
Bligh St
Mokonui St
Moana Cres
Te Anau Terr
Milford Rd
Jackson Rd
Pop Andrews Dr
Luxmore Dr
Bowen
Fiordland Cinema
Supermarket
Air Fiordland
ATM
Mokoroa St
Cleddau St
Quintin Dr
Henry St
Bev's Tramping Gear

Lake Te Anau

DoC Fiordland National Park Visitor Centre

Manapouri Te Anau Highway

To Queenstown

Wildlife Centre

To Ivon Wilson Park, Kepler Track, Airfield & Manapouri (20 km)

N

400 metres
400 yards

Where to stay 🛏
Fiordland Lodge 1
Te Anau Lake View Holiday Park 2
Te Anau Top Ten Holiday Park 3

Restaurants 🍴
Redcliff Café & Bar 1

Tunnel vision

Begun in 1935 and completed in 1953, The Homer Tunnel is a remarkable feat of engineering and a monument to human endeavour. It provides the essential link between Milford Sound and the outside world. When you first encounter the entrance to the Homer at the base of what can only be described as a massive face of granite, the word 'drain' springs to mind.

Ol'Homey has become the venue for perhaps New Zealand's most unusual annual events – known in these parts (no pun intended) as the 'Great Annual Nude Tunnel Run'. The race was originally conceived in 2000 and now attracts over 50 participants (including yours truly). Competitors run completely naked from east to west (a distance of 1.2 km) carrying little except a torch.

The fastest male and female runners have their names engraved on the trophy, which for men is Ken doll and for women a Barbie (naked and in a running position, naturally)!

For detailed regional information contact the **Fiordland i-SITE visitor centre** ① *Lakefront Dr, T03-2498900, fiordland.org.nz daily 0830-1800, winter 0830-1700*). It deals with all local information and serves as the agents for domestic air and bus bookings. Real Journeys is the largest of the regional operators and they have an office downstairs from the i-SITE (open daily summer 0830-2100). It deals with its own considerable scope of transport, sights and activity bookings including local sightseeing trips on Lake Te Anau (including the Te Anau Caves) and to Milford and Doubtful Sounds.

The DoC Fiordland National Park visitor centre ① *at the southern end of lakefront (T03-2498514, doc.govt.nz, daily 0830-1800, seasonal.* is the principal source for information, track bookings office and up-to-date weather forecasts. There is also a small museum and audio-visual theatre ($3).

While you are in Te Anau do not miss the short 35-minute film **Ata Whenua** or **Shadowland**, a stunning visual exploration of the Fiordland National Park screened regularly at the contemporary **Fiordland Cinema** ① *The Lane, T03-249 8812, fiordland cinema.co.nz, daily 1300 and 1730*.

North of Te Nau

SH94 The Road to Milford

The 117-km trip into the heart of the Fiordland National Park and Milford Sound via SH94 from Te Anau is all part of the world-class Milford Sound experience. In essence it is a bit like walking down the aisle, past the interior walls of a great cathedral, to stand in awe at the chancel and the stunning stained-glass windows above. This may sound like an exaggeration but if nature is your religion, then the trip to Milford is really nothing short of divine. Of course much depends on the weather. Ideally it should be of either extreme – cloudless, or absolutely thumping it down. Under clear blue skies it is of course magnificent, but many say that the trip through the mountains is better during very heavy rain. It is an incredibly moody place, so don't be put off by foul weather.

From Te Anau you skirt the shores and enjoy the congenial scenery of **Lake Te Anau**. At 56 km long, 10 km across at its widest point, and covering an area of 352 sq km, Lake Te Anau is the largest of New Zealand's southern glacial lakes. Although a matter of

Fiordland National Park

Fiordland National Park is 1.25 million ha and the largest of New Zealand's 14 national parks. It is 10% of the country, twice the size of Singapore and plays host to 0.06% of the population. In 1986 it was declared a World Heritage Area on account of its outstanding natural features, exceptional beauty and its important demonstration of the world's evolutionary history. Four years later, in 1990, Fiordland National Park was further linked with three others –Mount Aspiring, Westland and Mount Cook (Aoraki) to form the World Heritage Area of South West New Zealand. It was given the Maori name Te Waipounamu (Te 'the'/ Wai 'waters'/ Pounamu 'greenstone' or 'jade'). Hopefully we can rest assured that with such official labels and protection it will remain the stunning wilderness it is.

contention it is thought the name Te Anau is a shortened form of Te Ana-au which means the cave of the swirling water current. (There are caves so named on the western shore).

Head inland at **Te Anau Downs** (30 minutes). This is principally a boat access point to the Milford Track. Another 30 minutes will see you through some low-lying alluvial flats and meadows as the Earl Mountains begin to loom large. In late December the valley is a flood of colourful lupins that may look spectacular but are non-native and considered a rapacious and troublesome weed within the park.

After penetrating some beech forest and entering the park proper you suddenly emerge into the expanse of the **Eglinton River Valley** with its stunning views towards the mountains. This is known as the 'Avenue of the Disappearing Mountain' and it speaks for itself.

At the northern end of the valley you then re-enter the shade of the beech forests and encounter **Mirror Lake** a small body of water overlooked by the **Earl Mountain Range**. The lookout point is a short walk from the road. On a clear day you can, as the name suggests, capture the mood and the scene twice in the same shot.

Several kilometres further on is **Knobs Flat** where there is a DoC shelter and information/ display centre and toilet facilities. For much of the next 30 minutes you negotiate the dappled shadows on a near constant tunnel of beautiful beech forest before reaching **Lake Gunn**, which offers some fine fishing and a very pleasant 45-minutes nature walk through the forest. The copious growth of mosses and lichens here provide the rather unsubtle hint that the place can get very wet, very often!

From Lake Gunn you are really beginning to enter 'tiger country' as the road climbs to **The Divide**, one of the lowest passes along the length of the Southern Alps. Here a shelter and an assortment of discarded boots marks the start of the Routeburn and Greenstone/ Caples Tracks. The car park also serves as the starting point to a classic, recommended (three-hours return) walk to **Key Summit**, which looks over the Humboldt and Darran Ranges. Round the corner there is the Falls Creek (Pop's View) Lookout, which looks down the **Hollyford Valley**. Depending on the weather this will be a scene of fairly quiet serenity or one of near epic proportions as the swollen **Hollyford River** rips its way down to the valley fed by a million fingers of whitewater.

Following the river north is the Lower Hollyford Road and access to Lake Marian (1 km), a superb (three-hours return) walk up through forest and past waterfalls into a glacial hanging valley that holds the lake captive. A further 7 km on is the charming Hollyford (Gun's) Camp, and the Hollyford Airfield, important access and accommodation points for the Hollyford Track, the trailhead for which is at the road terminus 6 km further on.

The short 30-minute return walk to the **Humboldt Falls**, which again are spectacular after heavy rain, starts just before the car park.

Back on the main Milford Road the mountains begin to close in on both sides as you make the ascent up the Hollyford Valley to the 1200 m **Homer Tunnel**, an incredible feat of engineering, and a bizarre and exciting experience, like being swallowed by a giant drain.

At the entrance keep your eyes open for **kea** (native mountain parrots) that frequent the main stopping areas at either end of the tunnel. If they are not there, it is worth stopping a while to see if they turn up. Watching these incredibly intelligent avian delinquents go about their business of creating general mayhem in the name of food and sheer vandalism is highly entertaining. There will be plenty of photo opportunities and despite the obvious temptation DO NOT feed them. A parrot fed on white bread, crisps and chocolate is, obviously, a very sick parrot.

Once out of the tunnel you are now in the spectacular **Cleddau Canyon** and nearing Milford Sound. Instantly you will see the incredibly precipitous aspect of the mountains and bare valley walls. The rainfall is so high and rock and mudslides so frequent that the vegetation has little chance to establish itself. As a result the rainwater just cascades rapidly into the valleys. Note the creeks that cross under the road. There are so many they don't have names, but numbers. These all count up steadily to form the **Cleddau River**, which, at **The Chasm** (20-mins return), is really more waterfall than river, and has, over the millennia, sculpted round shapes and basins in the rock. From The Chasm it is five minutes before you see the tip of the altar of **Mitre Peak** (1692 m) and spire of **Mount Tutoko** (2746 m), Fiordland's highest peak. It's now only five minutes before your appointment with the Minister of Awe at the Chancel of **Milford Sound**.

South of Te Nau

Lake Manapouri
Driving into the small village of Manapouri 20 km south of Te Anau you are – depending on the weather – immediately met with stunning vistas across the eponymous lake. If it were anywhere else in the developed world, it would probably be an unsightly mass of exclusive real estate and tourist developments, but remarkably it isn't and instead seems quietly content to serve merely as an access point and see visitors off across the lake en-route to Doubtful Sound. There are 35 islands that disguise the boundaries of Lake Manapouri and at a forbidding 420 m it is mighty deep.

At the terminus of West Arm, and forming the main access point via Wilmot Pass to Doubtful Sound, is the **Manapouri Underground Power Station**. Started under a cloud of controversy in 1963 and completed eight years later it is the country's largest hydroelectric power station supplying 10% of the country's needs. A 2040 m (1:10) tunnel set in the hillside allows access to the main centre of operations – a large machine hall housing seven turbines and generators, fed by the water penstocks from 170 m above. What is most impressive is the 9.2-m diameter tailrace tunnel, which outputs the used water at the head of Doubtful Sound – an amazing 10 km from Lake Manapouri and 178 m below its surface. The power station can be visited as part of the Doubtful Sound package (see page 110).

Doubtful Sound
Doubt nothing, this fiord, like Milford Sound, is all it is cracked up to be – and more. Many who have made the trip to Milford feel it may be very similar and therefore not worthy of the time or expense to get there. But Doubtful Sound has a different atmosphere to

Milford. With the mountain topography in Fiordland getting lower the further south you go, and the fiords becoming longer and more indented with coves, arms and islands, Doubtful Sound offers the sense of space and wilderness that Milford does not. Doubtful is, after Dusky, the second largest fiord and has 10 times the surface area of Milford and, at 40 km, is also more than twice as long. It is also the deepest of the fiords at 421 m. There are three arms and several waterfalls including the heady 619-m Browne Falls. Doubtful Sound hosts its own pod of about 60 bottlenose dolphins that are regularly seen by visitors as well as fur seals and fiordland crested penguins. It is also noted for its lack of activity. Captain Cook originally named it Doubtful Harbour during his voyage of 1770. He decided not to explore past the entrance, fearful that the prevailing winds would not allow him to get back out; hence the name. Doubtful Sound is accessed via Manapouri. For tour operators contact the i-SITE visitor centre.

Many say Doubtful Sound is the best sea kayaking venue in New Zealand with the added attraction of its resident pod of dolphin.

The Southern Scenic Route
The Southern Scenic Route is a tourist-designated route that roughly encompasses the journey from Te Ana south and east to Invercargill and then north via the Catlins Coast to Dunedin. Beyond Lake Manapouri and Doubtful Sound, the highlights of this trip are the undeveloped windswept villages of the south coast, the small seaside resort of Riverton, Southland's stoic and much-maligned capital Invercargill, a certain signpost in Bluff, Stewart Island and the scenic splendour and wildlife of the Catlins Coast.

Manapouri to Invercargill
Still reeling from the highs of Fiordland's stunning scenery, your journey south could include the main drag of Vegas and still seem boring, so just accept that fact and sit back and enjoy the peace and quiet of the road. SH99 has to be one of the quietest main roads in the country and between Manapouri and Riverton it's unusual to pass more than half a dozen cars even in summer. Generally speaking you will encounter very little with two legs. Instead what you will see is paddock upon paddock of sheep.

Tuatapere 80 km south of Manapouri is considered the gateway to the southeast corner of the Fiordland National Park (not that there are any roads) and in particular the 53-km **Hump Ridge Track** ① *31 Orawia Rd, T03-2266739, humpridgetrack.co.nz, daily 0900-1700, winter Mon-Fri 0900-1700*, New Zealand's newest 'Great Walk'. On the first section of the Hump Ridge Track is the 36-m-high, 125-m-long Percy Burn Viaduct the largest wooden viaduct in the world. As well as that the former saw-milling and farming town and (mysteriously) self-proclaimed 'sausage capital' of the country has a few other notable local attractions, including some fine jet-boating operations up the Wairaurahiri River and Lake Hauroko, boasting the steepest lake-to-coast river fall in the country (W Jet, Clifden, T03-2255677, T0800-376174, wjet.co.nz).

A further 10 km south and SH99 reaches the coast at the evocatively named **Te Waewae Bay** then passes the windswept and tired looking village of **Orepuki**, before reaching Riverton. **Riverton** – or Aparima, to use its former Maori name – is the oldest permanent European settlement in Southland and one of the oldest in the country. Located on the banks of the common estuary formed by the Aparima and Purakino rivers, it was formerly a safe haven for whalers and sealers and was first established as early as the 1830s. Now having gradually developed into a popular coastal holiday resort, Riverton is a fine place to stop for lunch, a short walk on the beach, or even to consider as a quieter alternative base to Invercargill, only 42 km to the east.

Invercargill

ⓘ *The Invercargill i-SITE visitors centre is housed in the Southland Museum and Gallery Building, Victoria Av, T03-214 6243, southlandnz.com. Daily Oct-Apr 0900-1900, May-Sep 0900-1700.*

When it comes to aesthetics a lot has been said about Invercargill over the years and sadly (and undeservingly) much of it has been negative. Invercargill is not pretty. Let's be honest. Stuck at the very rear end of New Zealand and sandblasted by the worst extremes of the southern weather, even its climate and geography are against it. This is nothing new or unusual, after all Scotland (to which Invercargill and the region as a whole is so closely linked) is an entire country that suffers the same affliction. But for Invercargill there is

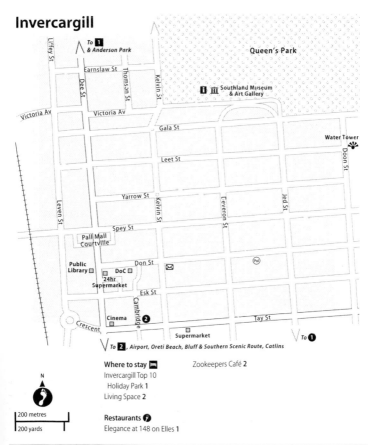

Invercargill

To **1** & Anderson Park

Queen's Park

Liffey St
Earnslaw St
Dee St
Thomson St
Kelvin St

ⓘ 🏛 Southland Museum & Art Gallery

Victoria Av

Victoria Av

Gala St

Water Tower

Leet St

Doon St

Leven St

Yarrow St

Kelvin St

Teveron St

Jed St

Spey St

Pall Mall
Courtville

Public Library □

□ DoC □

Don St ✉

24hr Supermarket

Pol

Esk St

Cambridge

Cinema □ **2**

Supermarket

Tay St

To **1**

To **2**, Airport, Oreti Beach, Bluff & Southern Scenic Route, Catlins

N

200 metres
200 yards

Where to stay 🛏
Invercargill Top 10
  Holiday Park **1**
Living Space **2**

Zookeepers Café **2**

Restaurants 🍴
Elegance at 148 on Elles **1**

one added problem. For most tourists the city features late on the travel schedule and by the time they get here they are almost drunk on stunning world-class scenery. No remedy there of course, it's an inevitable 'coming back down to earth', but were it not for the geography and the climate one cannot help but wonder if the problem could all be addressed with one weekend of frenzied mass tree-planting.

However, that said, Invercargill has many good points, and although you will hear different, it is certainly not the underdog it is reputed to be. For a start, it is the capital of the richest agricultural region in the South Island and serves admirably as the commercial hub of the region. Its people are also very friendly, welcoming and are the first to admit they have ten times the sense of humour of any North Islander.

Invercargill is a fine base from which to explore the delights of Southland and the Southern Scenic Route. Within a two-hour radius are a wealth of internationally acclaimed experiences of which Stewart Island, the Catlins Coast and southern Fiordland are the most obvious and the most lauded. So, by all means linger for a while – you won't regret it – and before you leave (while no one is looking) plant a tree!

The main highlight in the town is the excellent **Southland Museum and Art Gallery** ① *edge of Queen's Park, Victoria Av, T03-2199069, southlandmuseum.co.nz, Mon-Fri 0830-1700 Sat-Sun 1000-1700, donation*. It showcases all the usual fine Maori taonga and early settler exhibits and national and international art exhibitions, but is particularly noted for its Roaring Forties Antarctic and Sub-Antarctic Island display and audio-visual (25 minutes, $2) shown several times daily. Also excellent is the museum's tuatara display and breeding programme. The **Tuatarium** is an utter delight and an opportunity to come face to face with a reptilian species older than the land on which you stand. **Henry**, the oldest resident at an estimated 110 years plus, usually sits only a foot or two away from the glass. You can try to stare the old fella out, but you will fail, because Henry has had plenty of practice.

There are some good walking options around the city including those around Bluff or the huge 30-km expanse of **Oreti Beach** 10 km west of the city (past the airport). It has the added attraction of allowing vehicles (with sensible drivers) on the sand and safe swimming.

Bluff

Some 27 km south of Invercargill, the small port of Bluff heralds the end of the road in the South Island. Most visitors to Bluff are either on their way or returning from Stewart Island, or come to stand and gawk at a wind-blasted signpost at the terminus of SH1, which tells them they are several thousand miles from anywhere: next stop Antarctica.

The town itself is as strange as it is intriguing. As a result of a dying oyster-fishing industry and protracted general social decline, there is a very palpable sense of decay in Bluff. While the vast majority of New Zealand's other towns progress and grow at a healthy pace, here, it is as if the clocks have stopped and no-one's home. However, human creations aside, on the southern side of the peninsula the coastal scenery is stunning. There is no shortage of wind down here and the entire peninsula is sculpted accordingly. Bare boulder-clad hills shrouded in part with stunted wind-shorn bush and, on its leeward side, a surprisingly tall stand of native trees creates a fascinating mix of habitats. All well worth investigating along a network of fine **walking tracks**. The walks can be accessed from **Stirling Point** (road terminus) and you can climb to the top of **Bluff Hill** (Motupohue) at 270 m. From there you will be rewarded with fine panoramic views of the region and Stewart Island. The summit can also be reached by car from the centre of town (signposted).

Stewart Island (Rakiura National Park)

Tourist information For general information contact the **Stewart Island Visitor Terminal** ⓘ *Main Wharf, Halfmoon Bay, T03-2190034, T0800-000511, stewartislandexperience. co.nz.* Note this centre is owned and operated by Stewart Island Experience (a corporate body) therefore it is not an independent. For independent information consult the i-SITE in Invercargill. For national park tramping track, walks and latest weather information contact **DoC** ⓘ *Main Rd, Halfmoon Bay, T03-219 0009, doc.govt.nz.*

Lying 20 km southwest off Bluff, across the antsy waters of Foveaux Strait, is the 'land of the glowing skies' (Rakiura) or Stewart Island. Often called New Zealand's third island (making up 10% of its total area), Stewart Island was described over a century ago by pioneer botanist Leo Cockayne, as 'having a superabundance of superlatives'. There is much truth in that. It can be considered one of the country's most unspoilt and ecologically important areas. Such are its treasures that only the country's national parks can compare, which is why it was only a matter of time before it entered the fold in 2001, with 85% of the island now enjoying the limelight as the newest of New Zealand's 14 national parks.

The island is home to many threatened plant and animal species, some of which are endemic or occur only on the island. Although fighting to survive the ravages of introduced vermin, its impressive bird breeding list alone includes two of the rarest in the world: a flightless parrot called a kakapo (of which only about 80 remain) and perhaps most famous of all the Stewart Island brown kiwi, the largest and only diurnal kiwi in New Zealand.

The pleasant little village of **Oban** on Halfmoon Bay is the island's main settlement. It is connected to several smaller settlements including Golden Bay, Horseshoe Bay, Leask Bay and Butterfield Bay, by about 28 km of mainly sealed road. The rest of the island is remote, largely uninhabited and only accessible by boat.

Other than to see kiwi (which are usually only seen in remote areas), tours of the nature reserve of **Ulva Island**, boat trips, kayaking and diving, people visit Stewart Island for two main reasons: either to bask in its tranquility and do very little in Oban; or attempt one of its challenging, very long and at times very wet tramping tracks.

Catlins Coast

If you like remote and scenic coastlines you are going to love the Catlins, the added bonus here is their location. Like the Wairarapa in the southwest of the North Island, the area is generally off the beaten track and certainly underrated. You can negotiate the Catlins from the north or the south via the publicized Southern Scenic Route, encompassing a 187-km network of minor now fully sealed roads. The journey between Invercargill and Dunedin (or in reverse) is often attempted in one day, which is definitely a mistake. A more thorough, comfortable and less frustrating investigation will take at least two days, preferably three. But, if you can really only afford one day, the highlights not to be missed are: from the north, **Nugget Point** (for sunrise); the opportunity to see **Hookers sea lions** at **Cannibals Bay** (morning); the **Purakaunui Falls** and **Purakaunui Bay** (for lunch); then **McLean Falls**, **Curio Bay** and **Slope Point** in the afternoon.

The Catlins is noted for its rich wildlife and vegetation. Of particular note are the pinnipeds, or seals. The Catlins is the only mainland region where you can observe New Zealand fur seals, Hookers sea lions and Southern elephant seals in the same location. The region is also within the very limited breeding range of the rarest penguin on the planet – the **yellow-eyed penguin** (hoiho) – and the rare and tiny **Hector's dolphin**. Incredibly, with a little luck, all these species can be observed quite easily, independently and at relatively close range. The tracts of dense coastal forest that still remain are made up predominately of podocarp and silver beech (but Curio Bay is home to a scattering of petrified fossil trees that are over 180 million years old) and are home to native birds like native pigeon (kereru) and morepork (a small owl). The forests also hide a number of attractive waterfalls.

From north to south the main centres for services and accommodation are Kaka Point, Owaka and Papatowai.

The i-SITE visitors centre in Invercargill and Gore can also supply information about the Catlins. The free The Catlins booklet and the websites catlins-nz.com and catlins.org. nz are both useful. **Owaka i-SITE visitor centre and Museum** ① *10 Campbell St, Owaka, T03-4158371, catlins-nz.com, open Mon-Fri 0930-1300 and 1400-1600, Sat/Sun 1000-1300 and 1400-1600.*

Southland listings

For hotel and restaurant price codes and other relevant information, see pages 9-13.

⬤ Where to stay

Te Anau *p102, map p102*
$$$$ Fiordland Lodge, 472 Te Anau-Milford Highway (5 km north of Te Anau), T03-249 7832, fiordlandlodge.co.nz.
A purpose-built luxury lodge, built in the classic lodge style and commanding stunning views across the lake and mountains. Smart en suite guest rooms, 2 self-contained log cabins, quality restaurant and a large open fire. The high ceilings, full trunk pillars and huge windows add to the appeal. The owners also offer a wide range of guided excursions.
$$$-$ Te Anau Lake View Holiday Park, 1 Te Anau-Manapouri Highway (overlooking the lake on SH95), T03-249 7457, teanau.info, tracknet.net. Spacious with a wide range of options from new motel units, to cabins, powered sites and tent sites. Internet café, sauna and spa, Sky TV. The added attraction here, other than the modern facilities is the organization of activities and ease of tramping track transportation in conjunction with the in-house 'Tracknet' company.

Motor parks
$$$-$ Te Anau Top Ten Holiday Park, 128 Te Anau Terr, T03-2497462, teanautop10. co.nz. A multi-award winner and one of

the best holiday parks in the country. The facilities are excellent and well maintained. It lives up to its name as having a 'bed for every budget'.

Milford and Doubtful Sounds
p103 and p105
$$$ Real Journeys, T03-249 7416, T0800-656501, fiordlandtravel.co.nz. Offers a range of overnight options on Milford and Doubtful Sounds. On Milford there are vessels varying in size and options from multi-share accommodation to cabins. All meals and activities (kayaking) included.
$$$-$ Milford Sound Lodge, just off the Milford Rd about 1 km east of the airfield, T03-249 8071, milfordlodge.com. For the independent traveller this really is the only place to stay in Milford Sound.

Invercargill *p107, map p107*
$$ Living Space, 15 Tay St, T03-211 3800, T0508 454 846, livingspace.net. Excellent value modern studio rooms and 2- to 3-bedroom apartments right in the heart of the town. Facilities include a comfy movie theatre, full kitchen facilities and off-street parking.

Motor parks
$$$-$ Invercargill Top 10 Holiday Park, 77 McIvor Rd (northern edge of Invercargill off SH6), T03-215 9032, T0800 486 873, invercargilltop10.co.nz. By far the best option in Invercargill. Small, peaceful and friendly.

Stewart Island *p109*

$$$ Port of Call B&B and Bach, Jensen Bay, T03-219 1394, portofcall.co.nz. Set in an idyllic spot overlooking the entrance to Halfmoon Bay, cosy and friendly. It offers an en suite double and great breakfasts and views from the deck. There is also a self-contained bach (holiday house) offering plenty of privacy. In-house water taxi and eco-guiding operation, including kiwi-spotting.

$$$-$$ South Sea Hotel, corner of Elgin Terrace and Main Rd, Oban, T03-219 1059, stewart-island.co.nz. A fine place to stay if you want to mix with the locals and experience Stewart Island life. A mix of traditional hotel rooms (some with sea views) and self-contained motel units on an adjacent property. Obviously there is an in-house bar where all the action (or lack of it) takes place and a restaurant where you can sample the local delicacy – muttonbird.

Catlins Coast *p109*

$$$ Nugget Lodge Motels, only 2 km from Nugget Point and 6 km from Kaka Point, T03-412 8783, nuggetlodge.co.nz. 2 modern self-contained units sleeping 3 and 2 in a superb position beside the beach and overlooking the bay.

$$ Papatowai Hilltop Backpackers, Papatowai, T03-415 8028, hilltop backpackers.co.nz. An excellent place offering doubles with a great view (1 en suite) and dorm beds. Log fire, modern facilities, hot tub, bikes, canoes, internet and much more.

Motor parks

$$$-$ Mclean Falls Holiday Park and Motels, T03-415 8338, catlinsnz.com. Modern park at the southern end of the Catlins close to the Mclean Falls offering the full range of accommodation options from self-contained family chalets to rather pricey powered sites. Camp kitchen and restaurant/café on site.

$$-$ Kaka Point Motor Park, on the edge of the town on Tarata St, T03-412 8801, kakapoint@hotmail.com. Quiet place offering 2 cabins and sheltered powered/tent sites. Camp kitchen.

🍴 Restaurants

Te Anau *p102, map p102*

$$$-$$ Redcliff Café and Bar, 12 Mokonui St, T03-249 7431. Daily 1800-late. Small and intimate pub with open fire and restaurant (separate) offering some particularly good lamb and venison dishes.

Milford Sound *p103*

$$ Blue Duck Pub and Café, Waterfront T03-249 7657. Summer 0830-1700, bar 1100 till 'close' winter 0900-1630, bar 1630 till close. This is your only option for eating with a full range of pub-style food from generous breakfasts to toasted sandwiches. There are also lunch options on cruises.

Invercargill *p107, map p107*

$$$ Elegance at 148 on Elles, 148 Elles St, T03-216 1000. Closed Sun. The city's most intimate fine dining option. An open fire adds to the atmosphere. Try the local seafood, venison or whitebait.

$$ Zookeeper's Café, 50 Tay St, T03-218 3373. Daily from 1000-late. Crowned by its corrugated elephant façade this is the best café in town, with a nice atmosphere, good coffee and good-value evening meals.

🎭 Entertainment

Te Anau *p102, map p102*
Cinema
Fiordland Cinema, The Lane, T03-249 8812, fiordlandcinema.co.nz. Daily 1300 and 1730, from $10.

Invercargill *p107, map p107*
Cinema
Reading Cinema, 29 Dee St, T03-211 1555.

☼ What to do

Cruises

The majority of day cruises (from around $60) explore the entire 15-km length of the sound to the Tasman Sea, taking in all the sights on the way, including the waterfalls, precipitous rock overhangs, seal colonies and an underwater observatory. On the overnight cruises (see **Real Journeys**, below) you take in all the usual sights, but can enjoy an extended trip, meals, accommodation and other activities including boat-based kayaking. The main cruise companies on Milford Sound are:
Milford Sound Red Boat Cruises, T03-441 1137, T0800-264536, redboats.co.nz. Another major operator, offering similar cruises and rates to **Real Journeys** (below), but they have no overnight cruises. They also own and operate Underwater Observatory, which can only be visited with their cruises.
Mitre Peak Cruises, T03-249 8110, mitre peak.com. One of the smaller cruise operators offering a low-passenger number (smaller boat), nature-orientated day cruises, from $68.
Real Journeys, T03-249 7416, T0800-656501, fiordlandtravel.co.nz. The main cruise company operating on Doubtful Sound. Day (8 hrs) trip begins with a cruise across Lake Manapouri, then a ride by coach over Wilmot Pass to Doubtful Sound, a 3-hr cruise on the sound and a visit to The Manapouri Hydro-Electric Power Station on the return trip, from $245. Overnight trips are another option, from $263.

Kayaking

Fiordland Wilderness Experiences, T03-249 7768, T0800-200434, fiordland seakayak.co.nz. A wide range of excursions on both Milford and Doubtful Sounds. The Milford trip is especially good, taking in the scenery of the Milford Rd.
Roscos Milford Kayaks, T03-249 8500, kayakmilford.co.nz. Offers a range of day safaris and the standard paddle on the sound from Te Anau. Operates year round.

Road tours

Catlins Wildlife Trackers Eco-tours, Papatowai, T03-415 8613, catlins-ecotours. co.nz. Have been operating for more than 12 years and offers award-winning 3-day eco-tours (from $730), which explore the region's forest, coast, natural features and wildlife.
Kiwi Wilderness Walks, T021-359592, nzwalk.com. A popular operator that provides a range of multi-day guided eco-walks of Stewart Island with possibility of observing kiwi in daylight, an unforgettable experience. Recommended.
Trips and Tramps, T03-249 7081, T0800-305807, milfordtourswalks.co.nz. Locally orientated, personable road day-trips to Milford Sound and many other venues (including cruise and walking options).

☼ Transport

Invercargill *p107, map p107*
Invercargill has a domestic airport and also serves Stewart Island.

Stewart Island *p109*
Stewart Island can be reached by air (20 mins) from Invercargill to Halfmoon Bay or the western bays (trampers) with **Stewart Island Flights**, T03-2189129, stewartisland flights.com, from $195 return ($115 one way). There are scheduled flights 3 times daily.

The principal ferry and island tourism operator is **Stewart Island Experience**, T03-2127660 / T0800-000511, stewartislandexperience.co.nz, operates regular sailings from Bluff. The crossing by fast catamaran takes about 1 hr and costs from $71 one-way. The company offers a regular daily shuttle service to and from Invercargill to coincide with the Stewart Island ferries. Contact direct for latest schedules, bookings advised, T0800-000511. Secure outdoor vehicle storage is available at Bluff.

Contents

Footprint features

Footnotes

History of New Zealand

The first footprints

Due to its geographic isolation New Zealand was one of the last 'viable' lands to be settled by humans and therefore has a relatively young human history.

Though much debated and a simplification, Maori trace their ancestry to the homelands of 'Hawaiki' and the great Polynesian navigator Kupe, who is said to have made landfall in Northland, around AD 800. Finding the new land viable for settlement, Kupe named it Aotearoa – The Land of the Long White Cloud. Leaving his crew to colonize, Kupe then returned to Hawaiki to encourage further emigration. A century later the first fleet of waka (canoes) arrived in Aotearoa to settle permanently. It was the crew of these canoes that formed the first iwi (tribes) of a new race of people called the Maori.

The ancestral land called Hawaiki is thought to be Tahiti and the Society Islands, but exactly when and how these early Polynesians arrived and how they lived is in doubt. What is known is that they arrived sporadically in canoes and initially though struggling with the colder climate of New Zealand particularly in the South island, they persevered.

By the time the first European explorers arrived the Maori had developed their own culture, based on the tight-knit family unit and a tribal system not dissimilar to the Celts and Scots. In a desire to protect family, food resources and land the Maori, like the Scots, saw their fair share of brutal inter-tribal conflict. The Maori developed a highly effective community and defence system built within fortified villages or pa and cannibalism was also common. By the 16th century they had developed into a successful, fairly healthy, robust race. This period is known as the Classic Period. But despite the Maori successes in colonization, the subsequent environmental damage was dire and irreversible. A classic dynamic of cause and effect was set in place that would compromise the land forever. The Maori and the animals they brought with them (particularly dogs and rats) proved the nemesis of the unspoiled and isolated biodiversity of the land. Now, with the sails of European ships appearing above the horizon it was the Maori themselves who were facing the threat of annihalation.

European exploration

Although rumoured that the French or Spanish were actually the first Europeans to sight New Zealand, the first documented discovery was made in 1642 by Dutch explorer Abel Tasman. Tasman was sent to confirm or otherwise the existence of the hotly rumoured Great Southern Continent (Terra Australis Incognita) and if discovered, to investigate its viability for trade. Tasman's first encounter with the Maori proved hostile and without setting foot on land he fled to Tonga and Fiji. He christened the new land 'Staten Landt' which was later renamed 'Nieuw Zeeland'. It was Tasman's first and last encounter with the new land, but his visit led to New Zealand being put on the world map.

The next recorded European visit occurred with the arrival of the ubiquitous British explorer Captain Cook on board the Endeavour in 1769. It would be the first of three voyages to New Zealand. Cook's first landing, on 7 October in Poverty Bay (North Island) was eventful to say the least, with what proved to be a classic culture clash with the resident Maori. Ignorance and fear on both sides led to a mutual loss of life, but unlike

Tasman, Cook persevered and after further encounters managed to establish a 'friendly' relationship with the new people he called *tangata Maori* (the 'ordinary people').

European settlement and the clash of cultures

After news spread of the Cook voyages it did not take long for European sealers and whalers to reach New Zealand and rape the rich marine resources. By the 1820s the New Zealand fur seal and numerous species of whale had been brought to the verge of extinction. As the industries subsequently declined they were quickly joined or replaced by timber and flax traders. Others including adventurers, ex-convicts from Australia and some very determined (and some would say, much needed) missionaries joined the steady influx. Samuel Marsden gave the first Anglican sermon in the Bay of Islands on Christmas Day, 1814.

Inevitably, perhaps, an uneasy and fractious integration occurred between the Maori and the new settlers (or Pakeha as they were called) and, in tune with the familiar stories of colonized peoples the world over, the consequences for the native people were disastrous. Western diseases quickly ravaged over 25% of the Maori population and the trade of food, land or even preserved heads for the vastly more powerful and deadly European weapons resulted in the Maori Musket Wars 1820-1835. It proved a swift and almost genocidal era of inter-tribal warfare.

With such a melting pot of divergent cultures, greed and religion simmering on a fire of lawlessness and stateless disorganization, New Zealand was initially an awful place to be. Crime and corruption was rife. The Maori were conned into ridiculously unfavourable land-for-weapons deals and, along with the spread of Christianity and disease, their culture and tribal way of life was gradually being undermined. Such were the realities of early settlement that Kororareka (now known as Russell) in the Bay of Islands, which was the largest European settlement in the 1830s, earned itself the name and reputation as the 'Hellhole of the Pacific'. Amidst all the chaos the settlers began to appeal to their governments for protection.

The Treaty of Waitangi

By 1838 there were about 2000 British subjects in New Zealand and by this time the country was under the nominal jurisdiction of New South Wales in Australia. In 1833 James Busby was sent to Waitangi in the Bay of Islands as the official 'British Resident'. He was given the responsibility of law and order, but without the means to enforce it. Chaos reigned and finally, exacerbated by a rumour that the French were threatening to pre-empt any British attempt to claim sovereignty of New Zealand, Britain appointed Captain William Hobson as Lieutenant Governor to replace Busby. His remit was to effect the transfer of sovereignty over the land from the Maori chiefs to the British Crown. With the help of Busby who was now familiar with the ways and desires of the Maori, Hobson created what was to become the most important and controversial document in New Zealand history, the Treaty of Waitangi.

In the hastily compiled document there were three main provisions. The first was the complete cession of sovereignty by the Maori to the Queen of England. The second was the promise of full rights and possession of Maori lands and resources (but with the right to sell, of course). The third, and perhaps the greatest, attraction, given the chaotic environment, was the full rights and protection of Maori as British citizens. After two days of discussions, a few amendments and amidst much pomp and ceremony, over 40 Maori chiefs eventually signed the Treaty on 5 February 1840. With these first few signatures from the predominantly Northland tribes, Hobson went on a tour of the country to secure others.

To this day the Treaty of Waitangi remains a very contentious document. From its very inception it was inevitably going to be a fragile bridge between two very different cultures. Given the many differences in communication, translation and meaning, at best it was spurious or vague but worse still could, as a result, be easily manipulated in both actual meaning and subsequent enactment.

By the September of 1840 Hobson had gathered over 500 signatures, all in the North Island. Feeling this was enough to claim sovereignty over New Zealand he did so, and declaring the right of discovery over the South Island, made New Zealand a Crown Colony, independent of New South Wales and Australia. But the refusal and subsequent omission of several key (and powerful) Maori chiefs paved the way for regional disharmony and eventually war.

Maori (Land) Wars

In 1840 Hobson established Kororareka as the first capital of New Zealand, but given its reputation and history, he moved the seat of government to Auckland. With the increased influx of settlers, all greedy for land and resources, human nature very quickly superseded the legal niceties and undermined the fragile bridge of the new bicultural colony. In a frenzy of very dubious land deals between Maori and Pakeha (white settlers), as well as misunderstandings in methods of land use and ownership, resentment between the two was rife. This, plus the heavy taxes that were being demanded by the new and financially strapped government, strained the bridge to breaking point. The Maori were beginning to feel disenfranchised and began to rebel against British authority.

Legendary and belligerent chiefs like Hone Heke and Te Kooti (who for a time became the most wanted man in the land) put up a determined and courageous fight. But with far superior weaponry and organization the British quickly subdued the rebels. In return for their disobedience, and despite the treaty, they confiscated huge tracts of land. This land was then sold to new or already established settlers. By 1900 over 90% of the land was outside Maori ownership or control. They were a defeated people and, with little or no power and with continued integration, their culture was rapidly crumbling.

Natural resources, consolidation and social reform

Although development suffered as a result of the conflicts, timber, agriculture and gold came to the rescue. With the first discoveries made in the 1850s much of the economic focus shifted to the South Island and the seat of a new central (as opposed to provincial) government was moved to Wellington, which became the capital in 1876. The gold boom saw the Pakeha population grow dramatically and although it lasted only a decade, the infrastructures that it set in place paved the way for agricultural, timber and coal industries to quickly take over. In the agriculture sector alone, especially through sheep and dairy cattle, New Zealand was becoming an internationally significant export nation and prosperity continued. Towards the end of the 19th century the country also went through a dramatic and sweeping phase of social reforms. Well ahead most other Western nations, women secured the vote and pioneering legislation was enacted, introducing old-age pensions, minimum wage structures and arbitration courts.

But again, while the Pakeha prospered the Maori continued to suffer. Despite the Native Lands Act of 1865 that was established to investigate Maori land ownership and distribute land titles, by 1900 the Maori population had decreased to less than 50,000 and with the integration of Maori and Pakeha, pure Maori were becoming even more of a minority.

Prosperity and the world wars

By 1907 New Zealand progressed to the title of 'Dominion' of Britain rather than merely a 'colony' and by the 1920s was in control of most of its own affairs. By virtue of its close links with Britain, New Zealand and the newly formed (trans-Tasman) Australia and New Zealand Army Corps (ANZACs) became heavily embroiled in the Boer War of 1899-1902 and again in the First World War, at Gallipoli and the Western Front. Although noted for their steadfast loyalty, courage and bravery, the ANZACs suffered huge losses. Over 17,000 never returned with one in every three men aged between 20 and 40 being killed or wounded. Their First World War casualties remain the greatest of any combat nation.

After the First World War New Zealand joined the Western world in the Great Depression of the 1920s, but it recovered steadily and independently progressed in an increasing atmosphere of optimism. Again from a solid base of agricultural production it prospered and immigration, particularly from Britain, grew steadily. The population had now passed one million and it was enjoying one of the highest standards of living in the world.

Progress ceased temporarily with the outbreak of the Second World War and once again, the loyal ANZACs answered the call. With the spread of the conflict across the Pacific, it proved a nervous time for the nation, but with the dropping of the atomic bomb in Japan the threat ceased and the war was over.

New Zealand today

Post 1945

In 1947 New Zealand was declared an independent nation but maintained close defence and trade links with the Great Britain, the USA and Australia. In 1945 it became one of the original member states of the United Nations (UN) and later joined the ANZUS Defence Pact with the USA and Australia. Domestically, the country again prospered but the nagging problems of race relations, land and resource disputes between Maori and Pakeha still had to be addressed.

In 1975 significant progress was made with the formation of the Waitangi Tribunal, which was established to legally and officially hear Maori claims against the Crown. This method of addressing the problems continues to this day, but as ever, the misinterpretations of the treaty and its translation remain a major stumbling block.

New Zealand joined most of the developed world in the economic slump of the 1970s and 80s. In response to the economic decline, the government deregulated the country's economy, paving the way for free trade and New Zealand, like Australia, was beginning to see itself playing a far more significant role in the Asian markets as opposed to the traditional European ones.

One of the most important landmark decisions made on foreign policy in the 1980s was New Zealand's staunch anti-nuclear stand. In 1984 it refused entry to any foreign nuclear-powered ships in its coastal waters. This soured its relationship with the US who reacted by suspending defence obligations to New Zealand made under the ANZUS pact in the 1950s. This anti-nuclear stance is still maintained with considerable pride and is one that was only strengthened when the French Secret Service bombed the Greenpeace vessel *Rainbow Warrior* in 1985, causing national and international outrage. Relations with France were further soured in 1995 with the rather arrogant and insensitive testing of nuclear weapons in French Polynesia.

Throughout the 1990s the National Party continued successfully to nurture the free market economic policies first initiated by Labour. In 1999 the Labour Party were re-elected under the leadership of Helen Clarke. Her success as Prime Minister was to prove unprecedented, remaining in power until 2008 when Labour were ousted from government by the National Party under the leadership of new PM John Key.

The new millennium

Given its size and isolation New Zealand enjoyed considerable yet brief worldwide attention when on 1 January 2000 it was the first country to see the dawn of the new millennium. However, less appreciative attention was to follow after the infamous terrorist attacks of 11 September 2001 and the subsequent US-led military interventions in Afghanistan and Iraq. Unlike the Howard government of Australia, the New Zealand government led by Helen Clarke did not to align itself with that US policy and in a way repeated the fracas over the anti-nuclear stance of the 1980s. Most kiwis were very proud of Helen Clark's intelligent and (some say) truly democratic leadership at the time, despite the ramifications in current world affairs. The majority did not want to join the campaign in Iraq and its government rightfully and steadfastly exercised that voice. Kiwis are proud of their country and are more concerned about community and the environment than misguided patriotism, power and politics.

So returning to the shadows (bar the substantial hype surrounding the filming of Lord of the Rings) New Zealand remains a 'low-key' nation largely left to its own devices, blessed by an outstanding natural environment, healthy independence and the huge asset of a low and cosmopolitan population. It is not alone in its current economic struggles of course and a poor exchange rate and the ups and downs of free trade agreements may continue to cause problems as it did before the global financial meltdown.

Its biggest social challenge is the continued and difficult journey down the road of biculturalism as well perhaps as some sensible long-term decisions pertaining to future levels of immigration and eco-tourism. It also has its abiding and mutually respectful yet sometimes fractious relationship with Australia to deal with. But perhaps New Zealand's greatest challenge lies in the conservation and protection of its environment, for which it is most famous and much loved. Indeed, with a world facing the specter of rapid and human induced climate change perhaps it can – like Sweden – set an example for the rest of the world to follow. Dubbed the 'Clean Green Land' it certainly has a reputation to fulfill and an innate respect for environment is certainly there, but it remains to be seen whether its government and people can truly embrace the reality that its relatively healthy ecological condition is in fact probably due to its lack of population, as opposed to the common and traditional human attitudes that have proved to be so ruinous elsewhere.

New Zealand land and environment

New Zealand is a compact, diverse and ancient land that has been so isolated from any other land mass for so long that its biodiversity is described by some scientists as the closest one can get to studying life on another planet. Thanks to its long isolation, much of New Zealand's biodiversity is not only ancient, but endemic, with around 90% of its insects, 80% of its trees, ferns and flowering plants and 25% of its bird species, all 60 reptiles, four remaining frogs and two species of bat (the only native mammals) all found nowhere else on earth.

The 'Shaky Isles'

Given the fact New Zealand is located at the meeting point of the Pacific and Indo-Australian Plates, it is also a distinctly 'shaky' land of frequent earthquakes and constant volcanic activity. The Taupo Volcanic Zone in central North Island is one of the most active in the world. A string of volcanoes stretches from the currently active White Island in the Bay of Plenty, to the moody Mount Ruapehu in the heart of North Island. The area also has numerous thermal features including geysers, mineral springs, blowholes and mud pools, most of which can be found around Rotorua and Taupo. One of the largest volcanic eruptions in human history occurred in New Zealand in AD 186, the remnants of which is the country's largest lake – Lake Taupo. The most recent eruption occurred in August 2012 when Volcano Tongariro, which had been dormant for over a century, in North Island spewed out a huge ash cloud. The country's most dramatic earthquake in recent history occurred in Christchurch in February 2011; see box, page 24.

As a result of this volcanic activity, its associated geological uplift and the 'sculpturing' that has occurred gradually over the millennia, New Zealand's landscape is rich and varied. In the South Island glaciers, braided rivers, lakes, fiords (flooded glacial valleys) and sounds (flooded riverbeds) abound, while from Stewart Island in the South to Cape Reinga in the north there are alluvial plains, wetlands, large natural coastal harbours and a rash of offshore islands. Due to the 'uplift' created by the clash of the two tectonic plates, the South Island has many more mountain ranges than the North Island and boasts the country's highest peak, Mount Cook. Aoraki ('cloud piercer') as the Maori call it, stands less than 40 km from the west coast at a height of 3753 m. The country's longest river is the Waikato, which stretches 425 km from Lake Taupo to the Tasman Sea.

Wildlife

Although a mere echo of its former glory and ravaged by non-native (introduced) flora and fauna, modern-day New Zealand is still home to many endemic species. Your encounters will be many and memorable: from enchanting penguins to graceful albatrosses; cheeky keas to manic fantails, and rotund sea lions to breaching whales. Given the focus and fragility of its species, New Zealand is on the cutting edge of both conservation and ecotourism. As a visitor you will be able to experience both, working separately or in unison, and whether you love wildlife or are indifferent, you will be given a stark insight into our effect on the world and our place within it.

The following is just a mere sample of what you may encounter…

Vital statistics

New Zealand consists of three main islands – North Island, South Island and Stewart Island – with a handful of other small far-flung subtropical and sub-Antarctic islands. The total land area is 268,704 sq km (slightly larger than the UK).

New Zealand's boundaries extend from 33° to 53° south latitude and from 162° east longitude, to 173° west longitude, which results in a broad climatic range from north to south. It is bounded north and east by the South Pacific Ocean, on the west by the Tasman Sea and on the south by the great Southern Ocean. The nearest mainland is Australia, 1600 km west, which is roughly the same distance as New Zealand is in length. The country's highest mountain is Mount Cook (3753 m) and the longest river is the Waikato, which stretches 425 km from Lake Taupo to the Tasman Sea. The most northerly point of the North Island is Cape Reinga in Northland, while the most southerly point on the South at Slope Point. Slope Point is (surprisingly perhaps) 4831 km from Antarctica.

Birds

New Zealand does not have a huge bird list but what it does have is very special indeed. Of course, many species like the blackbird have been introduced, while others like the magpie paid a visit from across the Tasman and never left. But what truly belongs here is usually flightless, probably made Darwin over-excited and is certainly found nowhere else on the planet. Of course the great icon, the kiwi is a prime example. But before trying to summarize a creature of such delightful nonconformity, one should first consider the moa.

Moa were up to 3 m tall (the tallest avian ever) and looked a bit like an ostrich. There were around 11 species and they were very common. But sadly brains did not match the brawn. They had very little fear of anything and were flightless, so once the Maori arrived they were quickly hunted to extinction.

Of course though most have never heard of the moa, everyone has heard of a kiwi. They are to the avian world what the platypus is to the mammalian and the epitome of birdie weird. Flightless of course, they have no wings and their feathers are more like hairs. They are nocturnal and live in burrows. They have long whiskers almost like those of a cat, which, along with an acute sense of hearing and smell, are its ammunition in the hunt for food. It is the only bird with nostrils at the end of its beak and its egg-to-body weight ratio is legendary. The egg of a kiwi averages 15% of the female's body weight, compared to 2% for the ostrich. That's like giving birth to a prize pumpkin. Females tend to be larger than males and when it comes to the brown kiwi, the male tends to do most of the incubating. Now, how's that for weird? They mate for life, sleep for almost 20 hours a day (not weird at all) and live as long as 30 years. There are four living species, the brown kiwi, the little spotted, great spotted and the tokoeka. The brown is the most common species and the one you are most likely to see in captivity. The best and only chance the vast majority of visitors get to observe these quirky characters in one of the many darkened 'kiwi houses' scattered around the country. Some of the best are to be found at Kiwi Encounter in Rotorua, the DoC Wildlife Centre at Mount Bruce and Willowbank Wildlife Reserve in Christchurch (page 27). The tokoeka of Stewart Island are the only wild kiwi that can be seen during the day, which creates something of a tourist pilgrimage to try to see them (see page 109).

Of course the coast is never far away in New Zealand and it is home to some of the nation's avian royalty. The world's only mainland colony of royal albatross is a major

Birds of play

Ah yes, the notorious kea – possibly the most wonderful creature with wings. This highly intelligent, utterly entertaining avian delinquent lives high above the tree line, where it nests amongst rocks and feeds on just about anything edible. They are the only alpine parrot in the world. Forget about you finding them; if they are around they will find you. Nicknamed the 'cheeky kea' – thanks to their inherently inquisitive nature and extrovert behaviour – they are particularly fascinated by cars, rucksacks and shoelaces, or indeed anything that can be dismantled, demolished or eaten. To have a flock descend in the middle of your lunch break is a bit like an encounter with a class of unsupervised infants with severe behavioural disorders in a sweetie shop – out of control. I say children because that is truly how they behave and it certainly relates best to your subsequent reaction. They are so appalling, carefree and fun-loving that it is almost impossible not to just let them get on with it.

Along with the kea another notable bird of remote mountainous areas is the flightless takahe. They look like some congenial, prehistoric, purple chicken. Another ancient species once thought to be extinct; they were dramatically rediscovered in Fiordland in 1948. There is now an intensive breeding programme to attempt to secure their conservation, with only about 100 birds remaining in the wild and about the same again kept in captivity or on predator-free islands.

attraction on the Otago Peninsula, as are the twilight comings and goings of the yellow-eyed penguin, regarded as the rarest penguin species in the world. New Zealand is also known as the seabird capital of the world and a remarkable 70% of its total avian 'who's who' is pelagic (the global average is 3%). The list is long and includes mollymawks (which are similar to albatrosses), shearwaters and petrels.

Other notable seabird attractions include the colonies of gannets at Cape Kidnappers (near Napier, in Hawke's Bay) and on Farewell Spit, off the northern tip of the South Island.

Thousands of offshore islands are proving crucial to the conservation of the country's native wildlife. Many combine to form an invaluable flotilla of 'arks'; ultimately the only hope for many species. Once the Department of Conservation has eradicated formerly introduced predators like rats and possums, the remaining small pockets of resident birds, plants and animals are encouraged to re-colonize, and captive endemic breeds can be re-released. Some of the species that are now reliant on the 'arks' include birds like the kakapo (an ancient flightless parrot of which only 62 named individual remain), the kokako and takahe. To visit one of these vital reserves is to at least get a taste of the New Zealand of old and to experience the paradise lost. On one of these islands you enter a world of unique and ancient wildlife that shows little fear of humans, creating a near bombardment of the senses. The islands of Tiritiri Matangi and Kapiti Island off the Wellington coast are just two examples.

Tragically, like so much of the planet, New Zealand has now lost the vast majority of its natural forest cover. The impact on the whole ecosystem has been immense; most of the native forest that remains is confined to inaccessible areas and mountain slopes, with almost a quarter of that being in South Island's west coast region alone. The keruru (native pigeon), stitchbird, bellbird and the tui are all found in the lowland and forest habitats. The tui is quite common and you are bound to see, and certainly hear them. They boast a remarkable and entertaining range of whistles, grunts and knocks.

Of all the smaller birds encountered most folk's favourite is the enchanting little fantail. These charming little birds are a bit like butterflies on speed and your visit to New Zealand will more than once be enhanced by their inquisitive nature.

The kaka is one of New Zealand's three native parrot species. Once common throughout the country they are now confined mainly to old-growth forests. Although unmistakable in both call and plumage the average visitor would be lucky to see one in the wild, making your best bet the zoos or DoC wildlife centre at Mount Bruce in the Wairarapa.

Even tamer than the kaka but sharing its love for a free lunch is the weka, a flightless member of the rail family, often encountered at campgrounds and car parks and very often amid mass hysteria mistaken for kiwi.

Mammals

It is remarkable to think that New Zealand played host to only one mammal before we arrived, a small bat, of which two species (the long-tailed bat and the short-tailed bat) evolved. The vast majority of its biodiversity has wings, or lost the need for them through evolution and the lack of predatory, terrestrial mammals. Why the lack of terrestrial mammals? Well, around 23 million years ago New Zealand was mostly underwater. To what extent exactly is pure speculation, but estimates range from about 18% to the full 'Jacques Cousteau'. But this considerable dunking does explain why so much of what did become established or evolve did so as or from air or sea-borne immigrants – which of course eventually included us.

Sea mammals feature heavily. The tiny and endemic Hector's dolphin (again, one of the rarest in the world) joins many other species of dolphin and some fur seals, particularly around Kaikoura, which of course is also a top spot for whale watching.

In New Zealand today, besides the bat, there is now a thoroughly cosmopolitan and unsavoury list of terrestrial mammalian guests. This extraordinary list of reprobates includes the Australian brush tailed possum (an estimated 70 million – 20 to every person), stoats, weasels, hedgehogs, rabbits, hares, wallabies, ferrets, rats, mice, pigs, cats, horses, deer, goats and the entire cast of 'Big Brother' New Zealand. Combined we (and they) have become to New Zealand's native wildlife, what 'land-ahoy' did for the dodo.

Insects

New Zealand has an impressive range of creepy-crawlies, ranging from the noisy and the colourful to the downright bloodthirsty. There is even one the size of a mouse! But don't cancel your flight ticket just yet. By far the noisiest insect in the country is the cicada, which in summer and en masse can create an ear-splitting din in almost any area of bush or forest throughout the country. There are many species in New Zealand with one of the most common being the aptly named clapping cicada, though sometimes you wish a locust would pop by and tell them that the show's over.

But perhaps the most remarkable native insect in New Zealand is the weta, an ancient creature that has been around for millions of years. A number of species are found in gardens, forests caves and rock crevices throughout the country ranging from the common tree weta to the cave weta. But without doubt the most impressive is the giant weta. At up to 9 cm in length and weighing up to 80 g they are about the size of a mouse (Whooooah) and the largest insect in the world. Imagine one of those under the toilet seat (it's ok they don't do toilet seats!).

Of course, if you go anywhere near the west coast of the South Island you will become very intimate with the infamous New Zealand sandfly. What these wee creatures will do to source a feed of blood is the very epitome of motivation, tenacity and the combined tactical repertoire of both the RAF and Luftwaffe during the Second World War.

Reptiles and amphibians

To describe the noble and endemic tuatara as the most ancient reptile on earth is impressive enough, but when you consider that these living fossils are even older than the landscape itself, it seems truly remarkable that they exist at all. They belong to a very singular order of reptiles known as beakheads that once roamed the earth (be it very slowly) over 225 million years ago. Sounds very much like the House of Lords in the UK. Once common throughout the country, but subject to predation and a widespread loss of habitat, the tuatara, has sadly joined the long list of New Zealand creatures in decline and now exists on only on offshore islands. Given their status and natural habitat, your best chance of seeing a tuatara is in one of the country's zoos or museums. The Southland Museum in Invercargill is without doubt the most famous venue, having the most successful breeding and research programme in the world (see page 108). It also boasts perhaps the most famous tuatara in the land – 'Henry'. Henry is at least 110 years old – and guess what? After years of abstinence he has recently decided to once again take up that most desirable of pastimes – sex!

New Zealand's native frogs are also very old and very unusual. Called pepeketua they have hardly changed in 70 million years and have several distinctive features including no tadpole stage (young hatch from eggs almost fully formed and are then looked after by their parents) and they do not croak. There are also three introduced species of frog in New Zealand. One wonders if the natives go green with envy when they croak?

Flora

Like the country's animal life, much of New Zealand's plant life is beautiful, ancient and unique. Over 80% of the country's flowering plants are not endemic to any other land. But like the fauna, much of the country's plant life is in a worrying state of decline and tragically only about 15% of the New Zealand's original forest remains. The following are some of the most notable species that you are likely to see.

Alongside the iconic kiwi, the ponga or silver fern is New Zealand's other great national emblem and just one of a vast array of over 80 fern species. Depicted on everything from the national rugby jersey to the side of America's Cup yachts, the silver fern is a common sight in both the natural and commercial world. It is found throughout the mainly subtropical bush landscape, forming stands of almost prehistoric-looking umbrellas. A lush green colour on top, it is the silver underside that has created their notoriety.

Without doubt the most celebrated, yet overly utilized of the 100-odd forest tree species is the kauri. Occurring predominantly in the north of the North Island it was once the dominant tree of the region. With vast trunks often over 15 m in diameter, and 30 m tall, the kauri was prized by both the Maori for canoe building and by the early Europeans for masts and other shipbuilding materials. Sadly, over 90% of the trees were harvested and only a few ancient individuals remain.

New Zealand's best-known flowering tree is the beautiful pohutukawa; a gnarled-looking coastal evergreen that bursts into bright crimson flower for three weeks in December, earning it the affectionate label as New Zealand's Christmas tree.

Paradise lost?

New Zealand is often described as a natural paradise and given the isolation it enjoyed for millions of years it was just that, but on the day that man arrived, a mere 1000 years ago, it was not only 'paradise found', but was to become 'paradise lost'. Tragically, the 'introduction' of ourselves and all the non-native animals and plants we brought with us has caused more devastation to this clean green land than anything else in 80 million years of evolution. To say that the 'Land of the Long White Cloud' has been cast in to an abiding shadow of its former self would be putting it mildly.

In New Zealand today it makes the heart cry to experience the deathly hush of forests once alive to the sound of birds. At times it really is like standing in an ancient church that has been sacked of all its contents and robbed of both congregation and choir. Instead of a heads held high in celebration, the whispers of prayer and beautiful arias of worship, the pose is one of despair, the atmosphere one of remorseful reflection and the sound, one of eternal silence.

Although the country is often dubbed clean and green, many agree that it is far more a result of low population than attitude. As a result of our presence 32% of indigenous land and freshwater birds and 18% of seabirds are now extinct. Even the kiwi, the very emblem of the nation and its people is severely under threat and without more financing, it too is expected to be completely absent on mainland New Zealand within the next two decades. To lose the kiwi itself – the very bird after which its native humans are named – seems unimaginable.

Great efforts are being made in the war of conservation by the Department of Conservation, which as a funded governmental department is a rarity in itself. Independent organizations and eco-tourism also play a major role. Numerous captive breeding and predator eradication programmes have been initiated to stop, or at the very least slow down, the decline of so many species. Indeed, New Zealand is on the front line of the global conservation war and thankfully some battles are being won. But these battles all defy the shortsighted, financial and technologically driven society of the modern day. Since the very act of conservation is a drain on funds rather than a source, the DoC is always underfunded and until core values change it will be long and difficult climb towards salvation.

Index

BRANCH	DATE
JH	7/13

Titles available in the Footprint *Focus* range

Latin America	UK RRP	US RRP
Bahia & Salvador	£7.99	$11.95
Brazilian Amazon	£7.99	$11.95
Brazilian Pantanal	£6.99	$9.95
Buenos Aires & Pampas	£7.99	$11.95
Cartagena & Caribbean Coast	£7.99	$11.95
Costa Rica	£8.99	$12.95
Cuzco, La Paz & Lake Titicaca	£8.99	$12.95
El Salvador	£5.99	$8.95
Guadalajara & Pacific Coast	£6.99	$9.95
Guatemala	£8.99	$12.95
Guyana, Guyane & Suriname	£5.99	$8.95
Havana	£6.99	$9.95
Honduras	£7.99	$11.95
Nicaragua	£7.99	$11.95
Northeast Argentina & Uruguay	£8.99	$12.95
Paraguay	£5.99	$8.95
Quito & Galápagos Islands	£7.99	$11.95
Recife & Northeast Brazil	£7.99	$11.95
Rio de Janeiro	£8.99	$12.95
São Paulo	£5.99	$8.95
Uruguay	£6.99	$9.95
Venezuela	£8.99	$12.95
Yucatán Peninsula	£6.99	$9.95

Asia	UK RRP	US RRP
Angkor Wat	£5.99	$8.95
Bali & Lombok	£8.99	$12.95
Chennai & Tamil Nadu	£8.99	$12.95
Chiang Mai & Northern Thailand	£7.99	$11.95
Goa	£6.99	$9.95
Gulf of Thailand	£8.99	$12.95
Hanoi & Northern Vietnam	£8.99	$12.95
Ho Chi Minh City & Mekong Delta	£7.99	$11.95
Java	£7.99	$11.95
Kerala	£7.99	$11.95
Kolkata & West Bengal	£5.99	$8.95
Mumbai & Gujarat	£8.99	$12.95

Africa & Middle East	UK RRP	US RRP
Beirut	£6.99	$9.95
Cairo & Nile Delta	£8.99	$12.95
Damascus	£5.99	$8.95
Durban & KwaZulu Natal	£8.99	$12.95
Fès & Northern Morocco	£8.99	$12.95
Jerusalem	£8.99	$12.95
Johannesburg & Kruger National Park	£7.99	$11.95
Kenya's Beaches	£8.99	$12.95
Kilimanjaro & Northern Tanzania	£8.99	$12.95
Luxor to Aswan	£8.99	$12.95
Nairobi & Rift Valley	£7.99	$11.95
Red Sea & Sinai	£7.99	$11.95
Zanzibar & Pemba	£7.99	$11.95

Europe	UK RRP	US RRP
Bilbao & Basque Region	£6.99	$9.95
Brittany West Coast	£7.99	$11.95
Cádiz & Costa de la Luz	£6.99	$9.95
Granada & Sierra Nevada	£6.99	$9.95
Languedoc: Carcassonne to Montpellier	£7.99	$11.95
Málaga	£5.99	$8.95
Marseille & Western Provence	£7.99	$11.95
Orkney & Shetland Islands	£5.99	$8.95
Santander & Picos de Europa	£7.99	$11.95
Sardinia: Alghero & the North	£7.99	$11.95
Sardinia: Cagliari & the South	£7.99	$11.95
Seville	£5.99	$8.95
Sicily: Palermo & the Northwest	£7.99	$11.95
Sicily: Catania & the Southeast	£7.99	$11.95
Siena & Southern Tuscany	£7.99	$11.95
Sorrento, Capri & Amalfi Coast	£6.99	$9.95
Skye & Outer Hebrides	£6.99	$9.95
Verona & Lake Garda	£7.99	$11.95

North America	UK RRP	US RRP
Vancouver & Rockies	£8.99	$12.95

Australasia	UK RRP	US RRP
Brisbane & Queensland	£8.99	$12.95
Perth	£7.99	$11.95

For the latest books, e-books and a wealth of travel information, visit us at:
www.footprinttravelguides.com.

footprinttravelguides.com

Join us on facebook for the latest travel news, product releases, offers and amazing competitions:
www.facebook.com/footprintbooks.